Lessons I Hope You Have Learned

Life Lessons Passed Down From Your Grandparents

Dr. Joe Pettigrew

Lessons I Hope You Have Learned

FORWARD

We are excited to introduce Lessons I Hope You Have Learned. If grandparents could pass along a few lessons to their grandchildren, they wouldn't come from textbooks or lectures—they'd be lessons shaped by life, faith, and love. These are the principles you wish for them to carry as they grow, learn, and lead lives of meaning. It's not about grand gestures—it's in the everyday choices. It's in smiling at a stranger, offering forgiveness, or pausing to listen when someone feels unseen. The lasting impact of kindness will touch more hearts than you may ever know. Young or old, failure is a powerful teacher. It can feel like a dead end, but looked at through faith, failure often redirects us toward God's better plan. Lean into those moments, knowing that His strength is perfected in your weakness. You'll grow wiser, kinder, and more resilient than you could imagine. Our hope for our grandchildren isn't that they live a perfect life. It's that they live a life full of faith, love, and courage, holding onto the truth that God is with them every step of the way. Whatever storms may come, may they stand firm, rooted in the hope that can only be found in Him.

Joe

www.joepelligrew.org

Table Of Contents

How It Feels To Be Disappointed By A Close Friend 7

The Embarrassment Of Being Chosen Last 13

How To Be Truly Thankful 19

Older People Are Worth Listening To 23

That People Will Tell You, What You Want To Here 29

That Playing In The Rain Is Fun 33

What It Feels Like, To Be Lost In A Crowd 37

Many People Are Hungry, And Have No Money 41

Listening Is More Valuable Than Talking 45

To Put Things Back Where You Found Them 51

Being Happy, Is Your Responsibility 55

Grades Are Often Over Prioritized 59

People Will Break Your Heart 63

Do Nice Things For Strangers 69

Seeking Recognition Turns People Off 73

What's Important To Some, Is Not Important To Others 77

Your Family Is Important 83

Snow Days Are Special 87

There Is Always Someone, Smarter Than You 91

Pets Don't Live Forever 95

Making Mistakes Are Expected 99

Failing Is The Beginning, Not The End 103

How It Feels To Be Part Of A Team 107

To Make Time To Pick Up Seashells 113

How It Feels When You Fall Off A Bike 117

Some People Get Sick, And They Don't Get Well 121

Tomorrow Is Not Guaranteed   125

Everything, Is Not About You   129

Choose To Be Kind, Even When It's Not Easy   135

Finishing What You Start, Is Important   141

It's Easy To Make A Bad Decision   145

To Share, If You Have More Than Others   151

To Be Content, With What You Have   155

To Be Present, In The Moment   159

Look For The Best, In Everyone   163

To Admit, When You Are Wrong   167

How To Say, I Am Sorry   171

To Live For What Lasts   175

Make Time To Rest And Relax   179

To Remember, You Are Never Alone   183

Author   189

I HOPE YOU HAVE LEARNED

How It Feels To Be Disappointed
By A Close Friend

You think you know your friends. You think you understand almost everything about them. You have shared laughter and tears, secrets and dreams. In the quiet moments, you have been a shoulder to lean on, a voice of reason. Then, in an instant, you see the cracks. A broken promise, a thoughtless word, a moment of blatant selfishness. Disappointment. It's a heavy word, isn't it? Especially when it involves someone you trusted, someone you thought would always have your back. Maybe it was your best friend, your roommate, or that teammate you thought you could trust no matter what. And now, here you are, sitting with the sting of their words or actions, questioning everything.

It doesn't feel great, does it? Honestly, it feels kind of like having a surprise pop quiz in a class you didn't study for, except worse. Here's the truth no one tells you about disappointment in friendships. Every deep relationship you'll have in life will eventually involve hurt. Yeah, it stinks. But here's the other side of that coin–disappointment is often where the strongest friendships are tested, refined, and sometimes even rebuilt stronger.

Why does it hurt so much? Well, it's simple. The people closest to us hold the tools capable of building us up or cutting us down. Small things, like forgetting to text back or skipping your birthday dinner, might start to feel monumental because of the weight you gave them in your life. But you know what? Disappointment, as painful as it is, offers an opportunity for growth–for both you and your friend. Here are a few things we have learned (and honestly, still struggle to practice sometimes):

- You don't have to pretend you're "totally fine" when you're clearly not. Sit with your emotions, journal them out, talk to someone you trust. It's okay for it to hurt. It means you care.
- Ask yourself why does this hurt as much as it does? Did they cross a boundary you hadn't realized you'd set? Were your expectations not communicated as clearly as they needed to be? Understanding where the pain is rooted can help you figure out what to do next.
- This one is hard, I know. But the same way we've all screwed up with friends before (hello, who hasn't forgotten a birthday here or there?), they're human too. Sometimes disappointment comes not from ill intent but simple oversight.
- Yeah, it's awkward and sometimes terrifying. But a real friendship can stand up to a little honest conversation. Share how you feel without pointing fingers ("I feel hurt

when…" vs. "You always…"). Give them a chance to explain and maybe even repair things.

- After the air is cleared, you'll have a better idea of the friendship's foundation. Some will bounce back stronger. Others may reveal cracks you can't quite mend. And that's okay. Recognizing when to hold on and when to step back is part of adulting (ugh, adulting).

- It's so easy to slip into "I can't trust anyone" after being hurt by someone close. But people are complex– beautifully, frustratingly complex. And while one experience may leave a mark, don't allow it to stop you from opening your heart to others in the future.

Friendship is messy. It's filled with high highs and, unfortunately, some low lows. But learning to navigate those moments of disappointment can build resilience in ways you never expected. It may not be earth-shattering but something changes. There may be no dramatic confrontation, no screaming match to end all screaming matches. At first, you try to brush it off. Tell yourself you're overreacting, that everyone has a bad day. You begin to question if you really were as important to them as they were to you? Were all those shared moments real?

You deserve someone who will show up, not just in the big moments, but in the small ones too. Someone who will be a rock, not just when it's easy, but when it's hard. Someone who will see you, truly see you, even when it's inconvenient. Disappointment from a friend is a wound, yes. But like all wounds, it has the potential to heal, to leave you stronger on the other side. It forces you to reevaluate, to look at the relationships in your life with clear eyes. And sometimes, it pushes you to find friendships that are even deeper, more meaningful than you ever thought possible. Disappointment cuts deep when it comes from a close friend.

Even Jesus experienced this when Judas betrayed Him. Yet, Jesus teaches us to respond with grace and forgiveness, embodying love even in pain. Lean on God during these moments, for He understands your hurt and will provide comfort. Pray for strength to forgive and trust His plan. Rest assured, though people may fail, God's love never will. "*The Lord is close to the brokenhearted*" (Psalm 34:18). Find peace in Him. Disappointment from a close friend cuts deep, doesn't it? Even Jesus experienced this when Judas betrayed Him. Yet, in His pain, Jesus chose grace and forgiveness. Disappointments may come, but God's unwavering love and faithfulness remain. Trust Him to guide you through and bring peace to your spirit.

Advice From Someone That Loves You:

I want you to feel the ache of disappointment, but realize it's not the end. I want you to feel the weight of the fractured bond and realize sometimes it's time to move on. Please don't let disappointment define you. Instead, let it be a catalyst for growth, for finding the friendships that will lift you up, not drag you down. Because in the end, that's what true friendship is about. Not perfection, but a shared journey, a mutual lifting up, even in the face of disappointment. You have known what it's like to be disappointed by a friend. Your job now, it to make sure that you are not the person that disappoints others if you can possibly keep from doing it. You won't always be able to help people when and how they want. Sometimes what people want from you will not be in your best interest. I hope the disappointment you have learned will help you make the right decision.

And if you are currently feeling like your trust has been broken–you're not alone. We've all been there. The pain may not fade as quickly as we'd like, but in time, you'll find moments to laugh about again, build new bridges, and deepen the ones that truly matter.

Hang in there! Your heart? It'll heal. And when it does, it'll make room for even more beautiful, authentic connections. Being disappointed by a close friend has happened to us all. And it does hurt.

I HOPE YOU HAVE LEARNED

The Embarrassment Of Being Chosen Last

There's a particular sting to being chosen last. Most everyone has experienced it. You know that moment. The one where you're standing there, pretending not to care, hoping to be picked before you're the last person awkwardly lingering during a classroom or pick-up game selection. Everyone's eyeing up the "best choices," and meanwhile, you're staring at your shoes wondering if invisibility really is your superpower.It stings, doesn't it? Being picked last feels like a label stamped on your forehead that says, "Not enough." Not fast enough. Not smart enough. Not talented enough. But here's something to consider—that feeling of being overlooked could be exactly what you need to shape a brighter, more meaningful future. Think about it. Almost anyone who's done something incredible shares a similar story about being counted out. That sting of rejection, while painful, often becomes the fire that pushes you to grow and surprise everyone (including yourself).

It's a feeling that lingers for a long time-standing alone as teams are chosen. It's not just about the game, it's about the sense of not being wanted. Standing on the playground, waiting as the captains chose. The confident ones, the athletic ones, they're the first to be snapped up. The teams take shape, the clusters of kids dwindling until it's just you. Alone. There's a desperate scan, a hope that somehow you were overlooked. But all eyes are on you. The teams are even, except for that one empty spot. And you're the only one left. The walk to the team is agonizing. It's not about the distance, it's about the weight of all those eyes. You can feel the pity from those around you. You're not a choice, you're a necessity. The only one left. The captain looks at you, then back at their team. They don't want you, but they have no other option. "*I'll take...you,*" they say finally, the pause before your name a screaming indictment. The sting of being last choice isn't limited to childhood. It will happen again to you. A fear of not being enough, of always being an afterthought. It's there in the meeting, when ideas are being tossed around and yours is the last one considered. It's there in the social invitations, when you're the final one asked, the one they remembered only when they realized they had an extra seat. It's a hard feeling to shake, this sense of being an afterthought. But the only way to overcome it is to face it head-on. To remind yourself that your worth isn't tied to when you were chosen, or why. You are more than the teams you were or weren't picked for. You are more than the opinions of others. You have value, you have worth.

Here's the catch when it comes to being picked last. It can hurt now, sure. But it doesn't have the power to define you unless you let it. The truth is, whether you're picked first, last, or somewhere in the middle, there's more to your story than how others sort you into their own rankings. When you're chosen last, it's easy to feel small. Invisible. Forgotten. But being in that moment gives you something extraordinary. It teaches resilience. It builds empathy. It forces you to dig deep, get creative, and work harder to prove—even to yourself—that your worth doesn't depend on someone else's choice.

Sometimes being chosen last is the tipping point that leads to surprising victories. Think about everyone who's gone on to achieve something extraordinary after being "last." It wasn't because life handed them easy wins but because they didn't believe being overlooked was the end of their story. What if being chosen last didn't signal your weakness? What if it signaled root-building time? Picture a sapling that isn't quite ready to break the surface. Instead of growing upward, it digs deeper into the soil, finding strength and grounding itself for what comes next.

Here's how you can reframe it:

- No one moment defines your value. You decide where your story goes next.
- Getting picked last isn't your finish line; it's your start. Work to surprise people—not out of revenge, but out of a commitment to being the best version of yourself.

- It's easy to sulk about not being chosen, but don't waste energy being jealous or spiteful. Instead, champion those around you. Eventually, that positivity will circle back in ways you can't predict.

Next time you're not someone's first choice, remember this is the perfect setup for reshaping your identity, unlocking your potential, and building yourself into someone *you want to root for*. What feels like rejection now might actually be the moment you begin to discover your true calling. You're not defined by where *others* place you in the lineup—but by how you choose to grow from that very spot.

Advice From Someone That Loves You:

You may remember the feeling of being chosen last. Let it fuel you, let it drive you. When you are faced with having to make decisions that involve people, remember how you felt when you were over looked. Remember the embarrassing you felt. You will have to make some hard decisions but always remember there is a person involved in the other end of that decision. And that person has feelings just like you did. Remember, if they're going to underestimate you, you wanted to make sure that they regretted it. You wanted to show them what they overlooked. You wanted to show them the power of the one they chose last. There is always a way of helping people save face.

Imagine the look on those faces when the "last pick" ends up being the one everyone's talking about tomorrow. Exciting, isn't it? Time to go show up and prove that being chosen last doesn't mean you're out of the game. It often means you're just getting started. Being chosen last has happened to us all. And it does hurt.

I HOPE YOU HAVE LEARNED

How To Be Truly Thankful

Being thankful is a choice. It's easy to be thankful when things are going well, when life is falling into place. But the true test of thankfulness comes in the hard times, the times when gratitude feels like a distant memory. It's easy to get caught up in what's lacking, to focus on our struggles. And as you know, there will be struggles. There will be times when life is unfair. But in those moments, thankfulness is a choice. It's a mindset, a decision to focus on what you have, not what you don't have.

Let's talk about *being thankful*. Not the kind of thankfulness when someone hands you a slice of pizza, but the deeper, richer thankfulness that stays with you long after the moment has passed. If we're being honest, life can feel like a race. Classes, work, commitments, and that never-ending to-do list can make it hard to pause and feel grateful. And then there's the pressure to perform, to achieve, and to always have it "together." Sound familiar? But here's the thing about thankfulness—it's not about having a perfect life. It's about perspective. It's not about the *what*; it's about the *heart*.

True thankfulness isn't just a hashtag during the holidays or a quick "thanks" muttered out of obligation. It's a way of seeing the world. It's the realization that there's beauty even in the midst of chaos. It's that moment when you're sitting in a lecture and realize, "Hey, I may not love this class, but I'm lucky to be here learning." Or when you're wiping ketchup off your favorite hoodie and laugh because, honestly, it's just ketchup, and you've got more hoodies. Gratitude often comes in small, quiet moments. And sometimes, you have to work for it.

- Think of three specific things you're thankful for today. Not generic stuff like "family" or "friends"—get specific. Maybe it's the way your friend made you laugh during lunch or the playlist that hyped you up when you were working out today.

- It's so easy to dwell on everything that's going wrong or missing in your life. But what if you flipped the script? Instead of "I have so much homework," think, "I get to learn and grow my skills." Yes, it's hard sometimes, but reframing can shift your mindset.

- Your life isn't only made up of big, grand moments. It's also in the small joys—a warm bed, a kind text, or that first sip of coffee when your brain isn't awake yet. Those little sparks of joy add up, and they're worth celebrating.

- Gratitude isn't just for things. It extends to people too. Think about who's been there for you lately. A roommate, a professor, a classmate? Tell them. A simple "thank you" can mean so much.

Here's the wild part about thankfulness: it grows the more you practice it. It's like a muscle you intentionally work on. At first, it'll feel small or awkward or even forced. But over time, you'll see your perspective open wide. You'll notice the good more often, and suddenly, being thankful won't feel like a task. It'll feel like home.

Life in high school or college is chaotic, challenging, and sometimes downright frustrating. But it's *also* a time of learning, growing, failing forward, and figuring out who you're meant to be. Don't miss the good in all of it. Because trust me, there's so much good. Sometimes, you just have to look for it.

Being thankful will shift your thoughts. It helps you see that even in the darkest times, there is always something to be grateful for. It might be small, it might seem insignificant, but it's there. And it's those small things, those tiny sparks of light, that can guide you through the darkness. Being thankful doesn't mean ignoring the pain, it means acknowledging the good that exists alongside it. It means choosing to focus on the light, even as you navigate the dark. And it's that choice, that decision to be thankful, that can change everything. Thankfulness soothes your soul, calms your mind.

When you focus on what you're grateful for, you leave less room for worry, for fear. You create space for joy, for love. Choosing to be thankful will transform you. It can take the bitter and makes it sweet. It helps you see challenges as opportunities, not threats. It shifts your mindset, helps you grow. But most importantly, thankfulness is a choice. It's not a feeling that magically appears, it's a mindset you cultivate. It takes effort, it takes practice. But the rewards are immeasurable. Be thankful in all circumstances. Gratitude opens your heart to God's work and brings peace to your soul. Take a moment today to thank Him for blessings big and small. Trust in His plan with a grateful heart.

Advice From Someone That Loves You:

There have been many time we had to look for something to be thankful for when it felt like the clouds were closing in. There were even times when we failed to be thankful when we had everything going our way, including being a grandparent. Please, choose right now to be thankful. Thankful for everything you have, have had, and will have. Choose to focus on the good, to see the beauty in the everyday. Choose to be grateful, even when it's hard. Because in the end, it's not what happens to you that matters, it's how you respond. And a heart of thankfulness is the most powerful response of all. You may shock someone by how thankful you are. Some people rarely run across a person that is truly thankful. Let them see that you have so much to be thankful for, even when problems come your way. People love being around people that are thankful. Being thankful is important to us all.

I HOPE YOU HAVE LEARNED

Older People Are Worth Listening To

There's a beauty in age, a wisdom that only comes with getting older. Here's a question for you: When was the last time you had a real conversation with someone over the age of 70? Not just a quick "hi and bye", but an actual sit-down-lean-in-and-listen kind of conversation. We get it. You're just stepping into adult life, and it feels like the world is moving at 100mph. Life's exciting, chaotic, and brimming with issues that older folks "just wouldn't understand," right? But what if I told you that older people might just be the missing puzzle piece to whatever dilemma you're trying to solve?

Imagine this. You're stressing over all the things in life right now: your career, your love life, student loans, where you're going to live after college. Now think about this... older people have been through this already. They've faced heartbreak, financial worries, and job transitions. They laugh at the same existential freakouts you're having now because they've been there. And somehow, they made it through.

Guess what? That very experience you're so quick to brush off might just hold the insights you need. The wisdom they've gained doesn't come from some abstract place. It comes from living, failing, learning, and moving forward.

If someone told you that there's a book full of cheat codes for navigating adulthood, you'd grab it, right? Well, older people are walking, talking pages of life hacks. And they want to share those stories—but only if you're willing to listen. The best part? They're rooting for you. They want to see you succeed, so they'll dish out advice for free. Yes, their storytelling might veer off into tales of "back in my day" or long-winded explanations about their first car. But stick with it, because in those moments are life lessons waiting to be uncovered.

Here's another reason to listen to someone older than you: it's an act of respect. When you care enough to consult the wisdom of a generation before you, it's like saying, "What you've been through matters." You'd be amazed how connecting with someone over their experiences brings warmth and mutual understanding. Plus, who doesn't love hearing how much cheaper everything was in the '60s compared to your $6 cup of coffee?

- Give us a call or an older family friend, and just ask them about their favorite memory.
- Don't step into conversations with a "yeah, yeah, I already know this" attitude. Ask honest questions.
- Sure, technology and trends are wildly different now. But don't get hung up on those details. Dig for what's timeless.
- Whether it's a professor, coach, or neighbor, older mentors bring perspective that makes navigating life's challenges a little less overwhelming.

It might sound funny, but the more you listen to older people, the more you realize how much we all have in common. The same hopes, the same fears, and the same desire to feel like we're making a difference. Your professor who offered wisdom in office hours? The uncle sharing his "college survival" tips? The sweet lady down the street talking about her garden? They're all carrying something special they can teach you. You just have to take the time to hear it. So this week, find someone with a little more gray hair and a lot more experience, and lean in. You might be surprised how much their story changes yours.

Older people have lived through things you can only read about. They have experienced history firsthand. They've seen the world change, grow, shift. They've felt joy and pain, love and loss. And through it all, they've learned. But in our youth-focused culture, it's easy to overlook the value of older people. We forget that wisdom isn't found in years, but in experiences. And older people, have had a lifetime of experiences. Listening to older people is like reading a history book, but better. It's lessons learned, wisdom earned. And it can be invaluable to you.

They can tell you about the world as it was, about events that shaped history. They can share stories of how things used to be, of the ways society has changed. They can offer a perspective that textbooks can't, a firsthand account of the past. But it's not just about history. Older people have lived through all of life's stages. They've been where you are today. Thats hard to believe, but they were once your age and they have come out the other side. They've experienced the things you're experiencing, and they've learned from them. They can offer advice, guidance, wisdom. They can tell you what truly matters, and what doesn't. In a world that's always rushing forward, older people can offer a much-needed perspective. They can teach you that true happiness doesn't come from the latest trend, but from the people you love, the experiences you have. But you have to listen. You have to be willing to hear their stories, to learn from their experiences. You have to value their wisdom, their perspective. Because once they're gone, their stories are gone with them.

Advice From Someone That Loves You:

So, take the time. Sit with an older person, ask them about their life. Listen to their stories, learn from their wisdom. Show them that you value their experiences, their insights. Because older people aren't just worth listening to, they're essential. In an age-obsessed culture, it's easy to overlook the value of age. But wisdom isn't about years, it's about experiences. And older people, have had a lifetime of experiences. So, listen to them, learn from them. Because in their stories, you'll find wisdom that will change your life. I know what you are thinking, I have heard these stories so many times. And you are probably right, but just maybe they are saying these things to you because you didn't hear them the first time. Think what you have learned in your lifetime. Multiply that by four and then imagine what if that knowledge just went away. Listening to them may be more helpful to them, than to you. Older people are worth listening to. You will be surprised at their wisdom.

I HOPE YOU HAVE LEARNED

That People Will Tell You, What You Want To Here

People will tell you what you want to hear. They'll say the words that will make you happy, that will avoid conflict. They'll hide their true feelings, their real thoughts. They'll tell you what you want to hear, not what you need to hear. It's easy to fall into this trap, to only hear what we want to hear.

Ever heard that phrase, "You can't handle the truth"? Well, sometimes people don't bother giving us the truth. Instead, they tell us exactly what we want to hear. It feels good in the moment, like someone just handed you a double scoop of your favorite ice cream. But here's the problem—even if it tastes sweet, it may not be what we really need.

When you're making big decisions—whether it's choosing a college major, deciding on a career path, or saying "yes" to that last-minute road trip during finals week—there will always be people who want to keep you happy. Friends, family, even random acquaintances. They mean well. But sometimes their words are more about keeping the peace than giving you honest, truly helpful advice.

Here's the thing: You don't need a crowd of hyped-up cheerleaders telling you you're amazing. (You are, by the way, but hang on.) What you really need are a few close people who care about your growth enough to tell you what's real—even if it's uncomfortable. When we surround ourselves only with yes-people or choose to ignore honest feedback, we risk staying stuck. Imagine you're running a race but have blinders on about how far ahead (or behind) you really are. There's no way to adjust your pace or improve your strategy. Life's the same way. Without truth, growth becomes stagnant.

Sometimes, getting feedback that feels a little awkward is the best thing for us. Maybe someone tells you your goal to backpack through 10 countries while starting a new job sounds "a bit much." It's not because they don't believe in your adventurous spirit. It's because they care about you being realistic and thriving rather than burning out. Not everyone deserves a vote in your life. But some people? They've earned a front-row seat. Choose those who will both encourage and challenge you, even if it's not always what you want to hear. How do you know who these truth-tellers are? Look for people who:

- Show genuine care and respect for your dreams.
- Have walked through the challenges you're facing now.
- Are not afraid to ask tough questions or point out blind spots (with kindness!).
- These people will still cheer for you, but they'll also help you stay grounded.

At the end of the day, YOU are the one walking your path. Listen to different perspectives, but make sure your decisions align with your values, aspirations, and long-term vision. It's great to have encouragement, but don't forget to weigh advice with wisdom and discernment.

We all want to be liked, to be loved. We all want people to agree with us, to support us. So, we seek out those who will tell us what we want to hear. We surround ourselves with yes-men, with people who will never challenge us. But growth doesn't come from hearing what we want to hear. It comes from hearing what we need to hear. It comes from facing the hard truths, from being challenged. It comes from having people in our lives who will tell us what we need to know, not just what we want to hear. So, seek out those who will tell you the truth. Surround yourself with people who will challenge you, who will push you to be better. Don't just listen to those who will tell you what you want to hear. Listen to those who will tell you what you need to hear. It won't always be easy. It won't always be comfortable. But it will be worth it. Because the only way to truly grow, to truly improve, is to face the hard truths. Is to hear what you need to hear, not just what you want to hear. Be mindful of seeking only comforting words. True growth comes from hearing the truth, even when it challenges you. Surround yourself with people who'll guide you in His wisdom, not just what's easy to hear. God's love leads you towards greater purpose, even through correction.

Advice From Someone That Loves You:

Be open to hearing the truth, even when it's not what you want to hear. Surround yourself with people who love you enough to cheer you on and challenge you. That mix is the secret sauce to growing into the person you're called to be. And, by the way, if someone told you today, "You're doing a great job," that's the truth too.

Do you have people around you that will tell you what you need to hear? If not, you may want to get busy and find some. If you look around and find that most of your friends are sucking up to you because you like it, then realize that you are setting yourself up for trouble. Don't just listen to those who will tell you what you want to hear. Listen to those who will tell you what you need to hear. Because in the end, it's not about being happy in the moment. It's about being better in the long run. And that only comes from hearing the hard truths.

I HOPE YOU HAVE LEARNED

That Playing In The Rain Is Fun

Rainy days. They can be gloomy, gray, and depressing. Or, they can be an invitation to adventure, a chance to break free from the ordinary. Because playing in the rain can be fun. Who says you can only enjoy life when the skies are clear? College students and recent high school grads, this one's for you.

There's a unique kind of joy in stepping outside on a rainy day, isn't there? You know the feeling. The thunder rolls in, the skies open up, and instead of running for cover, you kick off your shoes, splash through puddles, and feel completely alive. It's messy. It's unpredictable. But it's also freeing. And isn't that what life feels like sometimes?

Rain can hit you unexpectedly. One moment you're strolling confidently through your day, and the next, a challenge comes pouring down like a surprise thunderstorm. Maybe it's balancing a heavy class schedule, navigating relationships, or figuring out what's next after graduation. Life doesn't always offer an umbrella. But rain isn't all bad, is it? Remember how refreshing it feels when it breaks a long heat wave? Rain nourishes, cleanses, and brings growth. Sometimes, it's our cloudy moments that prepare us for the brightest days ahead. That's where the fun comes in.

Why hide when you can dance in it? Rain-filled moments in life may feel inconvenient or even overwhelming, but they're also opportunities. Here's why you should take a minute to "play in the rain" when life pours down on you:

- When you learn to find joy in the uncomfortable, you grow stronger. You're saying, "This situation won't define me."
- When was the last time you embraced a challenge with laughter? Sometimes facing the storm head-on can spark unexpected moments of happiness.
- After the rain, the sunshine always feels warmer, brighter, and more appreciated.

This week, channel your inner kid. What's something in your schedule right now that feels "stormy"? A tough assignment? A job interview? Uncertainty about your major? Instead of seeing it as a downpour, what if you treated it as a chance to grow? Here's the challenge: Take one thing you're stressed about and find a way to look at it differently. Dance through it. Laugh at it. Find the lesson hidden within. Remember, most storms pass quicker than we expect. And who knows? You might just find that playing in the rain leaves you with a story to tell and a smile on your face.

Go on. Step outside. Splash around. Life is waiting for you—in sunshine and in the rain. Think back to your childhood. Do you remember splashing in puddles, feeling the cool rain soak through your clothes? Do you remember the smell of the wet earth, the taste of raindrops on your tongue? There was a joy in it, a freedom. We lose that as we get older.

We start to see rain as an inconvenience, something to be endured. We grab our umbrellas, our raincoats, and hurry to get out of the wet. But in doing so, we miss out on the fun. Because playing in the rain can still be fun, no matter how old you get. It's about embracing the child within you, about finding the joy in the simple things. It's about splashing in puddles, feeling the rain on our skin, and laughing with abandon. So, next time it rains, don't rush to get inside. Stop and embrace the rain. Stop and embrace the fun. Dance in the downpour, and let the rain wash over you. Because playing in the rain isn't just for kids. It's for anyone who wants to feel alive, who wants to embrace the joy of the moment.

Who doesn't need a little more joy in their life? Who doesn't need to feel carefree, to laugh with abandon, to remember the simple pleasures? We all do. And it's as simple as stepping outside on a rainy day, and embracing the fun. Playing in the rain reminds us of God's invitation to find joy, even amid life's storms. Like stepping into puddles, faith calls us to trust His plan and experience His peace. Don't fear the rain—embrace it, and discover the beauty God places in every moment.

Advice From Someone That Loves You:

Go ahead, the next time it rains just go outside and play. If someone asks you why, just tell them your grandparents suggested it. Splash in a puddle. Dance in the rain. And let the joy of the moment wash over you. Doing what we are suppose to do, gets boring and old. We often look at the rain as a bother rather than an opportunity. Playing in the rain isn't just fun it shows that you are not a stick in the mud and that having fun is important. It's a way to embrace life, to find happiness in the everyday. And that's something we can all use, no matter how old you get.

I HOPE YOU HAVE LEARNED

What It Feels Like, To Be Lost In A Crowd

Do you remember what it felt like to be lost when you were little? That feeling of utter terror, of the world spinning out of control? It's a unique kind of fear. A primal, heart-pounding dread. Because when you're young, the world is already a big, overwhelming place, and when you're lost, it feels even bigger, even more terrifying. You might have been in a crowded store, and turn around, and your parent is nowhere to be seen. Or you might be at a park, and wander a little too far, and suddenly you're alone. Or you might be on a trip, and get separated in the chaos of an airport. Wherever it happens, the feeling is the same.

Right now, you might feel unsure. Maybe you've moved away from home for the first time. Maybe your high school friends are scattered across universities and states, and you're wondering if you'll make friends like "them" again. Maybe it just feels overwhelming to think about how to find "your crowd" when everyone else seems to already have theirs. But here's something to think about: growth is often uncomfortable. When you plant a seed and water it, the growth doesn't happen in the open air first. It happens underground, where things are messy and invisible. That's kind of what you're experiencing right now. You're rooting, unseen. And soon, that growth will show itself in ways you didn't even realize.

Have you ever been at a concert, a sporting event, or even just wandering through a massive college campus, and suddenly felt... invisible? Being surrounded by thousands of people while feeling completely unnoticed can hit differently. It's strange, isn't it? You're in the middle of everything, yet it feels like you're nowhere at all. The truth is, crowds can be overwhelming. The pressure to feel connected, seen, or even relevant in a sea of strangers can weigh heavy, especially in college or just stepping into the real world after graduation. There's the voice in your head whispering "Shouldn't you belong somewhere? Shouldn't you have it all figured out by now?" But here's the thing you need to hear today. You're not the only one.

When you're in a crowd, it's easy to look around and think everyone else has it all together. But spoiler alert—not everything you see is real. That person who smiles like they have it all figured out? They've probably stared at their ceiling at 2 a.m. wondering where they're headed too. Feeling lost doesn't mean you're failing. It means you're human and in the middle of figuring things out. Even when it feels like the world forgot about you, you're still somebody with thoughts, dreams, potential, and value. Being lost doesn't take that away. Sometimes being in a crowd isn't about being noticed by others; it's about noticing yourself. The next time you feel swallowed up by life's chaos, try this:

- Stop scrolling, running, looking for ways to matter to someone else. Just pause and take a deep breath like you matter to yourself.
- You don't have to win a crowd's approval to have worth. (Sound cheesy? Sure. Still true? Absolutely.)
- Text a friend. Try a new hobby. Volunteer somewhere. Small, intentional steps build momentum when you feel stuck or invisible.

Your worth isn't determined by how loud you are in a crowd or how many people notice you. Some of the best moments in life often happen when no one's watching. Maybe the goal isn't to stand out or be remarkable, but instead, to show up for your story, one messy, beautiful step at a time. Because feeling lost doesn't mean being forgotten.

A jolt of fear, like a punch to the gut. Your heart races, your breath catches. You feel hot, then cold, then hot again. Your eyes scan the crowd, desperate for a familiar face. But all you see are strangers, looming over you like giants. You try to call out for your parent, but your voice is shaking, barely audible. Or maybe you're too scared to make a sound, frozen in place. You might feel tears prick at the corners of your eyes, a lump form in your throat. Because being lost as a kid, it's one of the scariest things there is. But even as you're afraid, there's a spark of determination in you. You know you have to find your way back, have to be brave. So you take a deep breath, and try to think clearly. The moment you see your parent's face, pushing through the crowd towards you.

The rush of relief, of joy. The tears of fear turning to tears of happiness as they sweep you up in a tight hug. Being lost as a kid, it's a traumatic experience. But it's also a formative one. It teaches you to be brave, to rely on yourself.

Advice From Someone That Loves You:

Few things are more scary than being lost. You remember I know a time when you were lost. You couldn't find anyone you knew and panic set in. And now, you are on your own now. You may need to take some risks and face some new challenges to prepare you for this world. It is in overcoming challenges that you will grow, that you will learn and thrive. And, don't give in to your fear if you get lost. Stay calm, think clearly, and always seek help. Because no matter where you are, you have the strength to find your way home. Next time you find yourself in the middle of it all, take a second. You're here for a reason, even if you can't see it yet.

I HOPE YOU HAVE LEARNED

Many People Are Hungry, And Have No Money

Alright, let's face it. Life post high school or during college is…well, complicated. You're suddenly juggling this whole "adulting" thing, trying to make sense of school, work, friendships, and maybe doing this all on a budget that barely covers ramen noodles. Sound familiar? For many, being "hungry and broke" isn't just a figure of speech. It's real. At some point, you might find yourself staring into your empty fridge, asking, "How did I get here?" Here's the good news (and yes, there's good news): this season of life might feel challenging, but it's shaping you in ways you can't even see yet. You're building resilience. Creativity. Gratitude for the small things. That's worth something.

This season of life might feel like you're stuck between wanting to pursue your dreams and needing a full meal that isn't cereal. And let's face it, the cafeteria of life doesn't often serve you what you ordered. But here's the thing: moments like these teach you grit, creativity, and that meals shared over laughter are richer than the fanciest dinners. When you can't afford the bougie café avocado toast, you learn to DIY it. Life's like that too. The challenges refine your resourcefulness. You don't have everything served to you, so you learn how to stretch what you DO have. Sometimes, the smallest blessings hit the hardest. That one free pizza at a club meeting? The neighbor bringing over extra cookies? Being broke teaches you to never take those moments for granted. You might be surprised how many people are willing to help when you're in need. Borrow a friend's couch when rent gets tough, accept their study snacks, or lean on that one classmate who shares a pack of gum like a saint. Lean into community. And equally, be there for others when you can. Generosity isn't about how much you have; it's about how much you're willing to pour into others.

Being broke and hungry isn't permanent. It's a part of the messy, beautiful tapestry of life that's teaching you one major lesson: life has layers. Some days will be peanut butter sandwiches; others will be steak dinners. Both have value. One day, when take-out orders are easy, and your fridge stays stocked, don't forget how it felt during those ramen days. It's this season of scrappiness that's helping shape the person you're meant to be. Stay encouraged, stay hopeful, and hey, maybe swap ramen flavors every week to keep things interesting.

Hunger and lack of resources are stark realities for countless people across the world. It's not just a distant issue —it's a struggle we might see in our own communities, in the eyes of a classmate skipping lunch or a neighbor quietly doing without. For young adults and college students, this reality can feel especially overwhelming. We witness these struggles yet often feel too stretched ourselves to make any meaningful impact. But even in these moments, there is hope, and there is action. You are called to care for one another. Helping those in need doesn't require vast wealth or grand gestures. Compassion and intention go much further than you might imagine. A $5 contribution to a local food pantry, sharing a meal with someone, or even simply sitting with someone who feels invisible can be an act of profound love. Small acts done with great care can make a tremendous difference in someone's life. Take a moment to evaluate how you engage in your daily life. Maybe it's being intentional when dining with friends by distributing leftovers thoughtfully. Perhaps it's creating awareness by organizing a food drive. These are not just acts of charity—they are acts of unity, linking you with the hearts of those around you. Lastly, hunger is not just physical.

Many people are yearning for connection, understanding, and hope. You have the power to fill those needs too. A kind word, a listening ear, or an invitation to join your table can satisfy a hunger that goes deeper than food. Never underestimate the impact that your presence and intentions can have on someone's life.

Advice From Someone That Loves You:

I hope you always have food, but you must remember that every night children go to bed hungry. That is not the problem of the government but it is also your problem. If you have—give it away. More than likely you have not been hungry as some often say. When you are down on your luck, it's a stressful, anxious, sometimes shameful feeling. But it's also a motivator, a chance to re-evaluate and rebuild. And with time, patience, and a lot of hard work, you will get back to a place where the buzz of anxiety fades, replaced by the satisfaction of stability. You can do this! Just don't forget that everyone is not like you. Parents in your own community listen to their children ask for food and can't give it to them. Don't blow that off, but look for ways of helping. I hope you never go hungry, just remember some are not that fortunate.

I HOPE YOU HAVE LEARNED

Listening Is More Valuable Than Talking

You have been taught that to be heard, you need to speak up. That participating in a conversation means expressing your own thoughts and opinions. While that's true, it's equally important to remember that we learn more by listening than by talking. Have you ever been in a conversation where it felt like both people were just waiting for their turn to speak? We've all been there. Maybe it was with a friend who wouldn't stop talking about their favorite Netflix show while you were trying to vent about a tough midterm. Or maybe it was you who had that amazing story about your recent trip and couldn't wait to share it. The thing is, talking comes naturally. But listening? That takes effort. And it's way more valuable.

When we actually stop and listen to someone, we're letting them know that what they're saying matters. We create space for them to be fully heard, and that can be incredibly powerful. People don't always want advice or solutions; sometimes, they just want someone to sit in the quiet with them and say, "I hear you." Think about the best conversations you've had. Chances are, they weren't the ones where you did the most talking. They were probably the ones where you felt understood, where someone really paid attention to what you were saying. Here's a fun fact you might not expect to hear about listening: silence is your superpower. Seriously. Have you noticed that when there's a pause in the conversation, a lot of people feel the urge to jump in and fill it? But when you allow that silence to settle, it gives the other person room to reflect, to dig a little deeper into what they're feeling or thinking. A lot can happen in that quiet space. It's where trust grows, where real connections form. Plus, it's a great way to avoid awkwardly cutting someone off mid-sentence (we've all been there, too).

Listening doesn't just happen. It's a skill, and like any skill, it takes practice to get better. Here are a few tips to help you become the MVP of listening:

- If the screen is lighting up with texts or TikTok notifications, you're not actually present in the conversation. Give the person in front of you your full attention.
- Show you're engaged by asking follow-up questions. "How did that make you feel?" or "What happened next?" can invite someone to open up more. It's not about interrogation; it's about curiosity.
- Sometimes, people just need to vent. You can't fix every problem (and you don't have to). Instead, try saying, "That sounds really tough. I'm here for you."
- Your posture says a lot. Lean in, nod, make eye contact. These small actions tell the other person, "I'm here. I'm listening."

- When you're formulating your next response while the other person is talking, you're not really listening. Practice staying in the moment instead.

Imagine how your relationships—with friends, family, classmates, or roommates—might change if you prioritized listening over talking. You might find yourself hearing things you've missed before. You'll probably notice people opening up to you more because they know you're someone who really cares about what they have to say. And here's a secret not many people realize until they practice listening for a while: when you become a great listener, people trust you more. They feel seen and valued. And when people feel valued… well, that's when relationships start to thrive.

Listening is how we gain new information. When we dominate a conversation, we're only sharing what we already know. We're not leaving space for others to impart their knowledge, their experiences, their perspectives. But when we take the time to truly listen –to fully absorb what the other person is saying – that's when the real learning happens. Listening also shows respect. When we give someone our full attention, when we ask open-ended questions and let them fully answer before responding, we're signaling that we value their thoughts. People are more likely to open up, to share more deeply, when they feel truly heard. And it's in those moments of vulnerability and trust that we often learn the most. We all walk around with preconceived notions, ideas about the world that may or may not be entirely accurate. But when we listen to others, especially those with experiences different than our own, we may find our assumptions shaken. We may realize that our view of the world is not the only view, and that can be a powerful catalyst for growth.

Listening doesn't mean agreement. We can listen to someone's perspective, can try to understand where they're coming from, without necessarily accepting their viewpoint as our own. In fact, sometimes the most growth comes from engaging with ideas that challenge us, that make us uncomfortable. As long as the conversation remains respectful, listening to opposing views can help us refine our own beliefs, or even change our minds.Listening opens doors that talking keeps closed. Take time to hear others—it's where wisdom, understanding, and connection grow. True growth often begins not with your voice, but in the silence where you truly hear. Quiet fuels clarity.

Advice From Someone That Loves You:

Conversations are a two-way street, and there's value in expressing your own thoughts and ideas. But in your rush to be heard, it's easy to forget the immense value of the quiet act of listening. Making a conscious effort to tilt the scales slightly more towards listening. You will open yourself up to new knowledge, deeper connections, and the chance to challenge your own assumptions. The next time you hear someone that wants to dominate the conversation, let them.

They need to do that. But the next time you find yourself
doing that, stop and remember, you really do learn more from
listening than from sharing your current knowledge. Talking
feels good. We all love a good rant or storytelling session. But
listening has the power to really change lives—not just the
lives of the people speaking, but yours too. Try it out this
week. The next time you're in a conversation, focus on
listening more and talking less. You might be surprised at the
connections you begin to build.

I HOPE YOU HAVE LEARNED

To Put Things Back Where You Found Them

It's a simple habit to get into, but one with profound implications: putting things back where you got them. It's a lesson you learned as a child, as people nagged at you to clean up your toys or return your books to the shelf. But as adults, it's easy to let this habit fall by the wayside. We've all heard this rule, haven't we? At some point in life, whether it was your parents or a well-meaning teacher, someone firmly reminded you to "put things back where you found them." Maybe it was about a pair of scissors, a book, or some random kitchen utensil that mysteriously wandered to the living room. But what if this simple, almost comically mundane rule applied to more than misplaced objects?

You see, life gets messy. College, new independence, first jobs, and figuring out who we are can feel like a whirlwind, shaking things loose in the process. And often, lost in all the noise, we forget to come back to things that ground us, things we didn't mean to set aside. Relationships are a great example of this. You're busy now. Maybe your phone is blowing up with group project texts, meme exchanges, or calendar notifications about yet another meeting. It's easy to forget to "put things back where you found them" when it comes to relationships—with family, friends, or even yourself. What happens when we don't? Over time, things drift. That friend who was always your go-to for venting has stopped texting. That conversation you planned to have with your sibling about their birthday feels long overdue. That quiet time to think or journal has somehow disappeared under a mountain of TikTok scrolls. Remember this rule, and try to return. Call that friend. Text your sibling. Pay attention to yourself. Why? Because putting things back where you found them isn't just about neatness. It's about preserving connections that matter.

Remember the things you used to love doing before schedules got so suffocating? Painting, hiking, cooking, playing that guitar collecting dust in the corner? Sometimes, we put these pieces of ourselves down just to balance everything else. And without realizing, life becomes all about juggling, not living. Pause and ask yourself what you've left behind. Return to it. Paint something, even if it's terrible. Take a walk and get soaked in creativity again. Reclaim the joy you once found in these pursuits.

This rule even applies to the small habits that keep us centered. Whether it's a moment of quiet in the morning, gratitude before bed, or connecting with friends who lift you up, put these habits back where you found them. They're essential, especially when life feels loud and overwhelming. Sure, this all started as a rule for misplaced objects. But it might just be your new favorite life motto. Sometimes all we need to do is pay attention to what we've lost along the way.

Relationships, passions, habits—we just need to pick them back up, return to what restores us, and adjust course. And that's how you take a simple rule about scissors and turn it into something surprisingly meaningful.

We get busy, distracted, and before we know it clutter starts to build up and a sense of disorganization takes hold. The simple act of putting things back where you got them can have a major impact on your productivity, your stress levels, and even your overall well-being. When everything has its designated place and you make a habit of returning items after use, you save yourself the frustration of the search. How many minutes have you wasted scanning the house for your keys or wallet, only to realize they were in your hand the whole time? When we put things back where they belong, we eliminate the need for those frantic searches. We can head out the door with confidence, knowing exactly where to find what we need.Putting things back where you got them also reduces clutter.

Clutter has a way of creeping up on us, a stray sock here, an unread magazine there, until before you know it your spaces feel overwhelming. But when you make it a habit to return items to their home, you prevent that buildup from happening in the first place. Your surroundings feel calmer, more peaceful, and are able to focus more clearly. This habit also promotes a sense of responsibility. When we take the time to put things back, we're acknowledging that we're the ones in control of our surroundings. We're taking ownership of our belongings and our space, rather than letting clutter and disorganization build up around us. That mindset can carry over into other areas of life, as we approach tasks and challenges with a greater sense of capability and self-control.Mistakes happen.

Things move, and priorities shift. But hey, you're not too far gone to reclaim what's been misplaced. Take a breath, refocus, and find joy in putting things back where they belong —even if it's just the ketchup in the fridge for now.

Advice From Someone That Loves You:

This is not new information for you. Remember all those times your parents told you to put your things up. If we are honest, we know that when we do that, it makes our lives easier. Putting things back where you got them will reduce stress, increase your productivity. So next time you reach for something, remember what you were taught and make a mental note to return it to its home when you're done. Your future self will thank you. For reference only, remember the frustration you had the last time you misplaced your keys.

I HOPE YOU HAVE LEARNED

Being Happy, Is Your Responsibility

We've all had those days where everything seems to be going wrong. The coffee spills on our clothes, the car won't crank, and to top it all off, it's pouring down rain. It's easy to let life's circumstances get you down, and to blame the world for your bad mood. But what if you could shift your mindset? What if you could take ownership of your own happiness, regardless of what the day throws your way?

Happiness. We all want it, talk about it, chase it...but how often do we stop to think, "Wait, who's responsible for it?" Here's the truth no one might have told you yet, but you need to hear loud and clear—*your happiness is up to you.* Not your friends, not your bank account, not your grades, or even that dream job you've been envisioning since eighth grade. You.

It's easy to blame external factors for how we feel. "I'd be happy if I had more money." "I'd be happy if my professor wasn't out to get me." "I'd be happy if I just had one clear direction in life." The reality is, waiting for circumstances to change in your favor before you allow yourself to be happy is like waiting for it to snow in Miami. It puts your happiness in someone else's hands. Here's the punchline (and the good news): While you can't always control what happens around you, **you can control how you respond to it.** You have the power to choose joy, even in moments where it feels like life is testing your patience (and trust me, it will).

Choosing happiness doesn't need to feel like an overwhelming task. Here are three ridiculously simple to-dos that anyone can try today:

- Ever start spiraling after a bad day? Maybe a small thing went wrong, and suddenly you're sure everything is falling apart. Stop those thoughts in their tracks. You don't have time for that kind of negativity. Instead, remind yourself of something (even one tiny thing!) you're grateful for. Perspective changes everything.
- Think of one activity that makes you lose track of time. (For me? It's crushing a bag of gummy worms during a Netflix binge. No shame.) Make time for that regularly. Whether it's art, sports, journaling, or a random hobby that makes zero sense to anyone else, do the things that fuel you.
- Laugh a lot. No really, it's science. Laughter reduces stress and releases feel-good hormones into your brain. Don't wait for life to hand you a reason to laugh. Watch your favorite comedian, tell a bad joke, hang out with that one friend who turns every situation into a comedy special. Find your funny.

Here's the deal. Life's not fair, the Wi-Fi will cut out at the worst possible moment, and people will have opinions about you that you can't control. Happiness doesn't mean ignoring reality; it means realizing that your mindset is not a victim of what's happening around you. You, yes YOU, have the ability to live with joy, even in the messy middle of figuring life out. You're not waiting for happiness to show up on your doorstep. It's already in your hands.

Happiness is a choice. It might not feel like it in the midst of a chaotic morning, but the truth is, you have the power to choose how you react to life's ups and downs. You can let the little annoyances pile up and steal your joy, or you can make a conscious decision to focus on the positive, to find the silver lining even in frustrating situations. You sometimes get stuck in a cycle of negativity, dwelling on what's going wrong rather than what's going right. The key is to become aware of that tendency, and make a conscious effort to shift your focus. Focusing on what we already have, rather than dwelling on what's lacking, is a surefire way to boost your mood and sense of well-being. In your busy lives, it's easy to put everyone else's needs first and forget to take care of your own. But the truth is, you can't pour from an empty cup. Taking time for activities that bring you joy and relaxation – whether that's reading a book, taking a walk, or practicing yoga – refills your tanks and sets us up to handle life's challenges with a clearer head and a lighter heart. Taking responsibility for our own happiness doesn't mean you will never have bad days.The key is not to beat yourself up over those feelings, but to acknowledge them, and gently nudge yourself back towards the positive.

Your circumstances won't always leave you smiling. Life doesn't promise easy days or guaranteed wins; it's often messy and chaotic and runs out of Oreos right when you need them. But your joy? That's something you can cultivate, regardless of what's happening around you. You're responsible for your happiness—not because it's always fun or easy, but because you're the only one with the power to grow it. Start small, give yourself grace, and breathe deeply knowing you've got this. Stay encouraged, and hey… go find something to smile about today.

Advice From Someone That Loves You:

I hope you are happy. I wish I could be there right now to do something special for you to make you happy. But being happy is your job now, not mine. It's a journey, not a destination. Some days will be easier than others. But with time and practice, you can develop the skills to choose happiness, even on the tough days. You can learn to focus on the positive, to practice self-care, and to find the lessons in life's challenges. And when you do, you will find that happiness is within your reach, no matter what the day brings.

I HOPE YOU HAVE LEARNED

Grades Are Often Over Prioritized

Grades – the letters or numbers stamped on your report cards, often seen as the ultimate measure of your success or failure in school. For many of us, grades feel like the end-all, be-all. If you ace that exam or finish the semester with a 4.0, you're winning. Right? But what happens when the A's don't come so easily? Or when you hit a wall and start questioning your own abilities? Suddenly, the number on a paper feels like a measure of your worth. Spoiler alert: **it's not.**

Here's the deal. While we're told from an early age that grades are the ticket to success, they're not the complete story. Sure, they show discipline and hard work, but they're not the only thing that defines who you are or who you're becoming. Your character, how you treat others, and your willingness to grow through challenges—that's what really sets you apart.Take a step back and ask yourself, "Why am I stressing over grades so much?" Is it because you genuinely want to learn, or is it the pressure to prove your value to others? Sometimes, we over-prioritize grades because we think they speak louder than who we are. But here's an honest truth many people *wish* they'd realized sooner in life: **You are more than your GPA.**

Grades often encourage memorization over understanding. Don't get me wrong, sometimes you've just got to know that formula or those definitions verbatim. (Shoutout to all the bio and chem majors!) But true learning happens when you engage your curiosity. It's about asking questions, making connections, and developing skills you can use beyond an exam room. Focus on absorbing knowledge— not just chasing perfect scores. Behind every grade is you growing in some way, even when the results don't look ideal. Did you struggle through that accounting class but finally understand how to map a budget? That's a win. Did you bomb a test but learn how to study better next time? Another win.

Here's the thing about balance: grades matter, but they're not everything. Stressing yourself into a sleepless spiral over school might lead you to burnout faster than anything else. Life isn't just about getting those marks; it's about becoming a well-rounded, fulfilled human being. What about taking time for hobbies, friends, or spiritual growth? Because here's the secret not many people talk about in college and beyond: finding fulfillment in who you are and the relationships you build *will* outshine perfect grades in the long run.

You're allowed to mess up. You're allowed to try your best and still not "get it." You're allowed to stumble and learn in the process. Instead of letting grades define who you are, focus on the type of person you're becoming. Are you compassionate? Are you resilient? Are you staying true to your values while working toward your goals? College (or life, for that matter) isn't just a place to earn grades. It's a time to figure out what you love, practice perseverance, and learn how to guide yourself through ups and downs with grace. You're on a path of growth, whether or not your transcript reflects it.

For many of us, grades loom large, determining how smart we feel and even our future career prospects. But is this emphasis on grades really that important, or has our focus on academic achievement led us to over-prioritize something that doesn't give us the full picture of a person's potential and worth? On the surface, grades seem like a logical way to measure your performance. But dig deeper, and it's clear that grades often paint an incomplete picture. Our intense focus on grades can have some unintended consequences. It can create a culture of competition rather than collaboration. When the goal is to earn the highest grade possible, students might be less likely to help their peers, share ideas, or work together on projects. Instead of viewing education as a journey of growth and exploration, it becomes a race to the top. But in the real world, success often hinges on our ability to work with others, think creatively, and adapt to new situations – skills that a singular focus on grades might not foster. The pressure to get good grades can also lead to significant stress and anxiety. You might feel your entire self-worth is tied to your GPA, leading to burnout as you study for hours on end, sacrificing sleep, health, and other activities you enjoy. The emphasis on grades can be damaging for mental health, particularly for those who don't fit the traditional mold of academic success. Rather than being the sole measure of success, grades could be one piece of a larger picture.

Advice From Someone That Loves You:

So you messed up your last test. Your life will never be the same. You will be a total failure forever. Really, don't go there. Please stop and think, is your focus on grades really doing justice to the wide range of talents, skills, and knowledge that you have. By broadening how you define success and expanding how you assess yourself, perhaps you can move beyond an over prioritization of grades and towards a more holistic view of education. Keep working hard but remember, grades are only one indicator of who you are and can be. Take a deep breath and repeat after me: **"I am not my grades."** You're here to learn, grow, and thrive—which doesn't always mean chasing perfection at every turn. Trust the process, do your best, and don't lose sight of the bigger picture. Oh, and for the times you need to laugh (or cry) about struggling through finals? That's part of the ride too. High-five your friends, grab some coffee, and remind yourself that you're doing better than you think.

I HOPE YOU HAVE LEARNED

People Will Break Your Heart

They were charming and attentive, showering you with affection and compliments. They were spontaneous, surprising you with sweet gestures. For the first time in your life, you felt truly seen and loved. But as the months passed, things began to shift. They would cancel plans at the last minute, barely offering an apology. They would forget important dates, then act like it was no big deal. The compliments that once flowed so freely became rare, replaced by critical comments about your appearance or choices. When you tried to talk about these changes, they would get defensive, telling you that you were overreacting. At first, you made excuses. You told herself they were stressed, that they didn't mean to hurt you. You tried to be more understanding, but no matter how hard you tried, it seemed like things only got worse. It took a painful conversation with a trusted friend to make you see the truth. Your friend pointed out the pattern – the initial infatuation, followed by a gradual pulling back. Looking back, you probably realized that they had broken your heart on purpose.

Life is full of messy, unpredictable relationships. If you're a college student or recent high school graduate, you've probably already realized this. People will break your heart, and it won't always be in a romantic way. It can come from a close friend flaking during a tough time, a family member letting you down, or someone you've trusted betraying you. It hurts, doesn't it? Like, *wow thanks for ripping my heart out with zero anesthesia* kind of hurt. But, you know what? It's also a part of what makes us human.

Pain in relationships, as awful as it feels in the moment, teaches us two crucial things. First, it reminds us that deep down, we care. We care about others, about connections, about the bonds that create community. Second, it strengthens our emotional muscles and shapes the way we show up for others.

You've been there, right? That gut-punch feeling of betrayal or disappointment when someone you trusted lets you down. Maybe it was a friend who ghosted you, a classmate who took credit for your part of the group project, or even a breakup that hit you harder than you expected. It's messy. It's painful. And it's… unfortunately, part of being human. But here's the thing no one tells you in the "Welcome to Adulthood" handbook (if only that existed, right?): People breaking your heart doesn't mean there is something wrong with you.

Truth bomb? It's not about you at all. It's about them. Their choices, their flaws, and their humanity. And trust me, you're human too. Yep, that means you'll probably disappoint someone at some point (gasp). But that doesn't make you unlovable or them unforgivable. It simply makes us all part of this beautifully imperfect, way-too-complicated thing we call life.

When people break your heart, it's tempting to build a fortress around it. However, if you don't allow vulnerability, you might miss out on truly meaningful relationships. Real connections don't come without a bit of risk, and that's okay.

Here's something to keep in mind:

- Not every heartbreak is about you. Sometimes, people hurt us because they're dealing with their own unresolved issues. That doesn't make it less painful, but it does help put things into perspective.
- You can forgive someone and still set boundaries. Forgiveness is about letting go of the bitterness, not pretending it never happened.
- Over time, you'll detect red flags sooner and value the people who treat your heart with care. The pain doesn't last forever, but your wisdom does.

Do you know what's even harder than heartbreak? When someone takes the last fries in a group meal without asking. See? Life's full of little betrayals too. (Okay, maybe not exactly the same thing, but still.)

If you're navigating a broken heart, remember this isn't forever. Your heart will heal, and you'll find new people who appreciate and love you for who you are. Trust me when I say those people are totally worth holding out for. Until then, give yourself grace. Cry it out if you need to, journal your thoughts, or binge-watch something that makes you laugh. And don't forget, breaking someone else's heart doesn't fix your own. Focus on kindness—to yourself and to others. Life will always bring people who test your patience and resilience, but remember, your heart's ability to bounce back is stronger than you know. You've got this.

They had drawn you in with their charm, just to pull the rug out from under you. It was a cruel game, one that left you reeling. But in the end, it is a catalyst for growth. You emerged from the experience stronger and wiser, with a deeper understanding of her own worth.

Honestly, if you think about it, no one should get away with breaking your heart and still having good hair days. But alas, life isn't fair, and we don't get that kind of cosmic justice. Instead, we have to pick ourselves up, laugh at the ridiculousness of it all, and keep going. People will break your heart. It's a fact of life. But it's also an opportunity to grow. The cracks they leave? Those are the places where light shines through. And as you move forward, continuing to learn, love, and connect, you'll find that the pain of heartbreak begins to fade, replaced with a deeper understanding of yourself, others, and what truly matters.

Advice From Someone That Loves You:

If someone has recently broken your heart, please provide me with your friend's address, I would like to meet him. Not really, but we certainly don't want to see get hurt. You will learn that sometimes, people will break your heart, not by accident, but as a conscious choice. They might do it out of their own brokenness, or as a way to assert power. But no matter the reason, it's up to you to recognize the pattern, to have the courage to walk away, and to heal in the aftermath. Because a heart that's been broken can always mend, emerging scarred but stronger on the other side.

I HOPE YOU HAVE LEARNED

Do Nice Things For Strangers

Starting small. Tomorrow buy an extra coffee and leaving it on the counter with a note that says, "Free coffee! Have a great day!" Hide in the background and watch, a surprised smile is all you need.The next day, pay for the order of the car behind you in the drive-thru. You will never see the person's face, but you can hear their delighted thanks to the drive through speaker.

Life can feel like a whirlwind, especially when you're navigating college or the post-graduate life. You've got classes, assignments, part-time jobs, internships, social obligations, and oh yes, figuring out how to be an adult for the first time. It's easy to get caught up in your own to-do lists and forget that there's a whole world of people around you, many of whom could use a small act of kindness. But here's the cool thing about stepping outside your bubble for a second to do something nice for a stranger: it doesn't just brighten *their* day; it can transform yours, too. Kindness has this weird, magical boomerang effect. It changes the atmosphere for everyone involved.

When you're kind to a stranger, it's a reminder for all of us that humanity, at its core, is good. Think about it. How many times have you been having "one of those days" only for someone to do something small, like hold the door open or give you an encouraging smile? That tiny moment of kindness stays with you, doesn't it? Now imagine being that for someone else. Kindness also teaches you to live in the moment. Do something nice for a stranger, and you'll feel connected to the bigger picture of life, even if just for a few seconds. It's like hitting the pause button on your own stress and allowing yourself to focus on something meaningful. You don't need to cure world hunger or rescue puppies from a burning building. Start small. Sometimes the tiniest acts of kindness go the furthest. Here are a few quick ideas to spark some inspiration:

- The next time you hit up Starbucks, leave an extra $5 to cover the person behind you.
- Seriously, we all love to be reminded of our swag. "Cool jacket!" or "Love your sneakers!" can go a long way.
- It's simple, but trust me, people appreciate it.
- Handwrite a thank-you note for someone who rarely gets recognized, like the janitor in your dorm or the barista at your regular coffee shop.
- Clean up your space. Whether it's wiping down a common table in your college library or picking up trash on the quad, acts of kindness can also be silent!

Here's the amazing part of doing nice things for strangers—it's not about getting something back, but you almost always leave with your own heart feeling fuller. You start to notice the goodness all around you. Kindness spreads, and chances are, the stranger you helped will pass it forward. This week, make it your mission to do something kind for a stranger. It doesn't have to be big or flashy; just a small moment of thoughtfulness will do. Who knows? You might just make someone's day... and make your own a little brighter in the process. Kindness is contagious. Spread it around wherever you go. Because in the end, the world doesn't just need more successful people; it needs more good ones. You've got this. Go brighten someone's day.

Consider carrying a stash of cards with you, write a short note and hand it out to a people you see doing something nice for other people. Some will look confused, but most will smile. You may find that doing nice things for strangers will shift your perspective. You me fill more connected to your community, more aware of the opportunities to make a difference in someone's day. Things like this can spark a sense of joy and purpose, even on the most mundane mornings.

Doing nice things for strangers may even become a hobby, your way of spreading ripples of kindness through the world. And as you go to sleep each night, just imagine where these ripples may travel, touching lives in ways you will never even know. Hold the door open. Compliment someone's outfit. Pay for the coffee of the person behind you. Small acts of kindness cost you little but can mean the world to someone else. Each time you go out of your way for a stranger, you're making the world brighter and living out love in action. Random kindness reminds us we're all connected. Today, find one moment to surprise someone with your kindness—you never know whose day you'll transform!

Life, especially as a college student or recent grad, can feel all about the hustle. Classes, internships, trying to figure out who you are and what you want to do... It's easy to get caught up in your own little world. But stepping out of that self-focused bubble to show kindness connects you to something bigger. Doing nice things for strangers also changes *you*. It reminds you to see others, to look up from your phone, and notice the world around you. It sharpens empathy, softens stress, and opens your mind to life outside your routine.

Advice From Someone That Loves You:

People in today's world just don't expect us to do nice things for people we don't know. That is so sad because I grew up in a day when that was considered something you were suppose to do for others. I hope you find that doing nice things for strangers isn't about grand gestures – it is about a mindset, a choice to see the humanity in every person you meet. It is about creating a world where kindness is the norm, one small act at a time. Look today for someone that you can make their day. It doesn't have to be something grand, just something kind.

I HOPE YOU HAVE LEARNED

Seeking Recognition Turns People Off

In a world that often measures success by likes, shares, and public accolades, the concept of doing things without wanting recognition can feel both foreign and freeing. At its core, this idea is about shifting our motivations. Instead of acting based on a desire for external validation, we focus inward. We find meaning and purpose in the act itself, rather than in the praise it garners. This mindset allows us to tap into a deeper sense of fulfillment, one that isn't dependent on the fleeting opinions of others.

Picture this: You're in a group project (groan, I know), and there's that one person who keeps inserting themselves into every detail, making sure to remind everyone how amazing their contributions are. "I came up with this idea," or, "Can we just appreciate the amount of effort I've put in?" We've all been there, right? And to be honest... it's exhausting. It's like they're running a one-person campaign for Most Valuable Team Member, and nobody's voting. Here's the hard truth—for many people, seeking recognition isn't inspiring; it's annoying.

It's human. We want to be seen, appreciated, and validated. Somewhere deep down, we think that if others don't notice what we're doing, it somehow doesn't matter.

But chasing recognition can lead us down this spiral of craving approval instead of focusing on doing genuinely good work. At its core, it's a distraction. And guess what? People see right through it. Now flip the script. Think about the people who inspire you most. Chances are, they aren't bragging about their accomplishments or constantly seeking pats on the back. They're the ones who quietly put their heads down, work hard, and make a difference without feeling the need to broadcast it to the world. Real impact doesn't need an announcement. When you do good just for the sake of doing good, without worrying about applause, people *will* notice. And more importantly, you'll feel a sense of fulfillment that no Instagram like or team acknowledgment can provide.

It's okay to want validation sometimes. But remember, your worth isn't tied to how loudly your contributions are noticed. The right people will see your effort without you needing to shout about it. Focus on your character, not just your achievements, and you'll leave an impression that matters far beyond any moment of applause. Think about this the next time you're tempted to fish for compliments or beam a metaphorical spotlight on yourself. Sometimes, the most powerful thing you can do is simply to show up, work hard, and trust that the results will speak for themselves. And hey, life isn't a race for recognition. It's about building something real, something lasting—with or without the round of applause.

Imagine creating art, not for the praise of critics or the admiration of crowds, but because the act of creation brings you joy. Picture helping those in need, not to be hailed as a hero, but because their struggles resonate with your heart. Envision pursuing a goal, not for the applause at the finish line, but for the growth you experience along the journey. Doing things without wanting recognition is a path that requires self-awareness and introspection. It demands we ask ourselves honest questions: What truly drives me? Is it the desire to make a positive impact, or is it the craving for approval? Am I attached to outcomes, or can I find contentment in the process? This isn't to say recognition never comes, or that it's inherently bad. Acknowledgement can be a wonderful thing. But when it becomes our primary motivator, we risk losing touch with our authentic selves. We may shape-shift to meet the expectations of others, rather than staying true to our own values and passions.Doing things without wanting recognition can lead to more meaningful recognition in the long run. When our actions stem from a place of genuine purpose, rather than self-seeking, they often resonate more deeply with others. They carry a power and sincerity that cannot be manufactured for the sake of applause.

The antidote to seeking recognition isn't to downplay your accomplishments or stay silent in the background. It's all about balance. Consider this:

- If your classmate aces an assignment or your roommate gets into grad school, take a moment to celebrate them.

Recognizing other people's wins shows that you're confident enough to uplift others. Bonus? They're much more likely to celebrate yours too.
- When you talk about something you're proud of, focus on sharing the genuine excitement behind it—not just fishing for likes or applause. People love authenticity.
- Shift the spotlight off yourself every now and then. Ask others about their lives, their passions, their stories. It's amazing how much stronger connections become when we simply take an interest in the people around us.

Here's the wild part about recognition. The *most meaningful* kind often comes when we're not even looking for it. When you work hard, stay consistent, and treat others well, people notice—even without a highlight reel. And that kind of respect? It lasts way longer than empty applause.

Advice From Someone That Loves You:

Doesn't it bother you when people brag on themselves. They tell you everything they did great and really expect you to be impressed. It often gets old. People just don't want us to talk about ourselves and how great we are. I hope you create, love, help, and grow for the sake of the act itself. In doing so, you will find a more lasting sense of purpose and fulfillment than any amount of external praise could ever provide. Remember, you don't need to receive your accolades from yourself. If you truly made a difference it will come out.

I HOPE YOU HAVE LEARNED

What's Important To Some, Is Not Important To Others

Recognizing that what is important to some is not important to others is a key part of understanding and appreciating human diversity. It's a reminder that we each have our own unique perspectives, shaped by our distinct life journeys and personal values. This difference is the spice of life. It allows for differing interests, passions, and contributions. If we all prioritized the same things, the world would be a dull and uninteresting place.

Have you ever been absolutely obsessed with something, only to realize no one else cares as much as you do? Maybe it's the perfect Spotify playlist you've spent hours curating, only for your best friend to skip through half the songs. Or that late-night taco place you're convinced is heaven on earth, but your roommate shrugs and says, "It's okay." Truth bomb: What's important to you isn't always going to be important to everyone else. And that's totally okay.

Here's the thing about life—we're all wired differently. We come from different schools, families, interests, and priorities. Think about how you light up talking about your favorite TV show, yet your parents still haven't figured out how to turn on Netflix. Or how you might value a quiet study session, while your group project partner wants to "crank the vibes" at a coffee shop blasting indie rock. Life isn't about forcing others to share your perspective or feeling dismissed because they don't. It's about learning to understand each other's quirks, passions, and priorities while staying true to your own. Here's some food for thought as you step into another day of balancing passions, perspectives, and personal identity:

- Your values and interests make you, well, *you*! Whether it's your love for photography, your dream startup idea, or your obsession with trivia nights, own what matters to you. These are the things that fuel your energy and creativity.
- Just like you want your friends to celebrate your passions, take time to discover what drives the people in your life. Showing interest literally costs nothing, but it can build a deeper connection. Maybe you'll find out why your friend's cactus collection is *actually* cool (or maybe not—but at least you tried).
- You don't need a cheerleading squad to prove your goals matter. Whatever's placed on your heart has purpose, even if it doesn't make sense to the people around you. Love what you love and keep going after it.
- You don't have to connect with *everyone*. Seek out the ones who get you or are willing to learn about the things you care about. Whether it's friends, mentors, or classmates who share your work ethic or interests, these relationships can carry you far.

Here's the takeaway, whether you're navigating finals, friendships, or figuring out your next steps in life. Everyone has their "thing"—different but equally meaningful. Give yourself the space to honor what's important to you, and grace for what may be important to others. And who knows? Maybe one day, you'll find someone who loves your favorite taco spot as much as you do.

Imagine if everyone shared the exact same hobbies, the same career aspirations, the same ideas of how to spend time. Progress and innovation thrive on the diversity of what people deem important. When we interact with others, it's easy to assume they share our priorities, simply because they feel so similar to us. But when their actions and decisions don't align with what we find important, conflict can arise. We might judge them, or feel judged in return. Yet, this is where the opportunity for growth lies. By recognizing and respecting these differences, we can deepen our empathy and broaden our worldviews. We can learn to appreciate the beauty in what others find important, even if it doesn't resonate with us personally. We can become more well-rounded individuals, with a greater understanding of the many facets of human experience. We all value different things, and that's okay. What feels urgent to one person might seem trivial to another. Understanding this can help us build stronger relationships and foster empathy. Pause and consider: what might someone else care deeply about that you've overlooked? Taking the time to listen and value another's perspective shows love and respect. It's not about agreeing on everything, but about understanding that we all walk different paths and hold unique priorities. Today, look for a moment to appreciate what matters most to someone else—it might just deepen your connection.

You never know what someone is dealing with on their own. That stranger you pass in the library or sit next to in a lecture hall might be carrying the weight of something you can't see. Your kind gesture might feel like a tiny drop in the ocean, but you have no idea how big those ripples could be in their life. Think of kindness like planting a seed. You might not see the tree grow—but trust that your action mattered. Alright, your turn. Go shine a little light out there today.

Have you noticed that what's critical to you might barely register as meaningful to someone else? It's subtly fascinating, isn't it? Whether it's your type of music, your favorite TV show, or how passionately you rank burgers over tacos (real talk, though, tacos are undefeated)—our priorities shape how we see the world.

This realization can hit especially hard in college or right after high school. You've entered a new phase where you're surrounded by diverse people from different backgrounds, all bringing their quirks, values, and perspectives to the table. Suddenly, what seemed universally important back in your small high school bubble (like being on the debate team or winning Prom King or Queen) kind of fades in comparison to newer challenges, goals, or friendships.

But here's the fun part: This diversity in values and priorities isn't a bad thing.

Advice From Someone That Loves You:

What is important to one person is not important at all to the other. You probably know someone that is eat up with fancy foods, but not me. They may never miss a sporting event on television, but not me. They may spend their weekends fishing, but not me. I hope you choose to celebrate the diversity of what individuals find important. I hope you seek to understand, rather than judge, when others prioritize differently. In doing so, you will build more compassionate connections and a more inclusive group of friends.

I HOPE YOU HAVE LEARNED

Your Family Is Important

In the hustle and bustle of modern life, it's easy to let quality time with our family fall by the wayside. It's easy to take family for granted, especially when you're caught up in the chaos of late-night study sessions, juggling part-time jobs, or figuring out how to cook something other than ramen (Hang in there, you'll get there). Family falls into the background as you focus on friends, fun, and keeping up with your crazy college schedule. But here's the thing – your family is important, even when they don't seem cool or totally "get" your TikTok obsessions.

Whether they're biological, chosen, or a mix of both, family is one of the few constants in your life. They're the people who were there when you were rocking braces and questionable haircuts, and they'll likely still be there after you figure out who you really want to be. They're the ones who cheer you on when life is good and rally around you when things are not-so-great. That kind of support? Rare and priceless.

Sure, families aren't perfect. They can be annoying. Like, "Mom texting 27 times to ask if you're eating enough vegetables" annoying. Or "Dad sending memes that stopped being funny five years ago" annoying. But they love you in a way that no one else does.

Your family knows the real you, not just the person you're trying to become. They can (and will) call you out when you're getting too full of yourself. Whether you're acing your finals or flunking them, they care. They're one call away —even if you're ugly crying over a grade, break-up, or the fact that your favorite pizza place no longer delivers.They remind you where you came from and give you something solid to lean on as you dream about your future.

You don't have to send a scroll-worthy "I miss you" letter or shower them with elaborate gifts to stay connected. Here are a few simple ways to show your appreciation:

- **Text First:** Break the habit of waiting for them to reach out. Send a quick "Hey Dad, remember when I tripped on stage at graduation? Good times."
- **Call... Yes, Call!** It doesn't have to be an hour-long talk. A five-minute chat can reassure them you're still alive and eating real food.
- **Laugh Together:** Share a funny meme, remind them of an inside joke, or just laugh about that one time Aunt Carol fell in the fountain. Laughter strengthens connections.
- **Say "Thank You":** A simple "Hey, thanks for helping me figure out my budget" or "Thanks for dealing with my panic about dorm life" goes a long way.

At the end of the day, these relationships matter. Make the effort. Life is unpredictable, and you don't want to wake up one day wishing you'd done more to appreciate the people who love you. Your family is important. And so are you. Don't forget to remind them of both. Go ahead, text your mom now. You know she'll love it.

Work or school obligations, social commitments, and personal pursuits can consume your schedule, leaving little room for the people who matter most. Yet, prioritizing family time is essential for both our individual well-being and the health of our relationships.First and foremost, family time nurtures the bonds that connect us. Shared experiences, laughter, and meaningful conversations strengthen the ties between grandparents, parents, children, and siblings. These moments of togetherness create lasting memories, a sense of belonging, and a support network that can weather life's challenges.

When you make time for family, you communicate that they are valued and loved, fostering a deep sense of security and trust. Family time also plays a critical role in shaping your values and identity. The time you share with loved ones exposes you to their perspectives, traditions, and ways of being in the world. These influences help mold your beliefs, interests, and sense of self. Beyond the emotional benefits, family time has been shown to have numerous positive effects on our well-being. Regular time with loved ones can reduce stress, improve mental health, and increase feelings of happiness. Shared activities promote social connection, which is vital for your overall health. In an era of increasing isolation, prioritizing family time is more important than ever. Of course, finding time for family can be challenging. Schedules conflict, interests diverge, and the pull of other obligations is strong. Yet, it's the consistent effort to connect that matters. This might be a weekly dinner, a game night, a weekend outing, or simply a commitment to put away devices and be present with one another. Even small moments of togetherness can have a profound impact.

Advice From Someone That Loves You:

I hope you have already figured out just how important family is. When everyone turns away from you, your family will be there. They know your faults and they still love you. As the old adage goes, *No one ever said on their deathbed, I wish I spent more time at work.* At the end of the day, it is the time and love you share with family that brings the greatest joy and leaves the most lasting legacy. So, please make the effort to prioritize family time.

I HOPE YOU HAVE LEARNED

Snow Days Are Special

There's something undeniably special about waking up to find the world transformed by a blanket of snow. There's something magical about snow days. No alarms, no classes, and for a brief moment, the world feels like it hits pause. For college students and recent high school graduates, that unexpected freedom can feel like the ultimate VIP pass to chill.

Maybe it's a chance to sleep in after pulling an all-nighter, or maybe it's the perfect excuse to binge-watch your favorite show guilt-free. Whether you use the day to catch up on homework, or build questionable-looking snowmen outside your dorm, snow days are nature's way of giving us a much-needed breather. But what makes snow days truly special is the reminder that sometimes, life throws us tiny moments of joy when we least expect them. When schedules are canceled and the pressure eases, take a moment to just enjoy it. Go out, laugh, slide on the ice (hopefully not too hard), and breathe in the crisp air. Your to-do list will still be there tomorrow, but today? Today was made for cocoa and cozy socks.

Whether you spend it being productive or just soaking it all in, don't overthink it. Snow days are life's little "just because" gifts.Ever notice how snow days feel like the universe hitting the "pause" button? For one glorious day, everything slows down. Deadlines become whispers instead of shouts. Classes, schedules, meetings, and to-do lists? All gone, buried beneath a blanket of white. It's like Mother Nature herself is saying, "Chill. Literally."

For college students, snow days are basically golden tickets. No exams, no group projects, no awkward elevator small talk in your dorm. Just you, some cozy layers, and that magical crisp air that makes everything feel softer and quieter. But here's the thing—not everyone gets these little gifts in life. Snow days are rare, even fleeting. It's tempting to pack all your unproductive habits into the day like a burrito of lazy, but there's an opportunity here to make it special.

Imagine using that free time not just for another Netflix marathon (although, love that energy), but for something that resets you. Sleep in? Absolutely. But maybe you also finally make that hot chocolate recipe with marshmallows you've been craving since middle school. Build a snowman? YES. Crush someone in a snowball fight? Double yes. Snow days remind us that it's okay to step away, to breathe, and to reset. You don't have to feel guilty for taking that break. The world didn't stop spinning because you slowed down for a second.

Because here's the truth about snow days, both literal and metaphorical: They're about making space. Space to laugh, to relax, to give yourself a break from the pressures of "go, go, go." Not every day will give you that permission, so when it does, lean in. Enjoy the beauty of the unexpected pause, and maybe even allow yourself to build something out of the moment. Snow days are special. Will you make the most of the next one?

The ordinary becomes extraordinary as the mundane is replaced by the magical. And for many of us, the first thought that comes to mind is, *Is this a snow day?* The possibility of a day free from obligations, a day to embrace the wonder of the season, is an exciting one. For children, snow days are the ultimate adventure. The thrill of hearing that school is cancelled, of knowing a day of play awaits, is unmatched. Memories of bundling up in warmest layers, of rushing outdoors into the crisp, cold air, stay with us for a lifetime. The snowball fights, the snowmen built, the hours spent sledding down the biggest hill you could find – these are the moments that make childhood so special.

There's a unique peace that comes with a snow day. The world feels quieter, as if muffled by the layer of white. The usual rush and hustle is replaced by a stillness, an invitation to slow down and appreciate the beauty around us. A snow day is a rare opportunity to unplug, to put aside our usual worries, and simply be in the moment. And then, of course, there's the joy of indoor activities on a snow day. The warmth of the inside is a cozy contrast to the chill outside. Hot chocolate warms our hands as we gaze out the window at the snowfall. Days spent reading by the window, watching the flakes gently fall, are days of perfect tranquility. As the day winds down, snow days often end with a sense of contentment. There's a sense of gratitude for this unexpected gift of a day. A snow day reminds us to appreciate the little things, to find joy in the everyday, and to never lose sight of the magic that can be found in the world around us.

Advice From Someone That Loves You:

I know you remember those nights when you were getting ready for bed and the weather reporter said, tomorrow is going to be a snow day. It was bigger than winning the lottery. It was beautiful, but it was fun. I hope you always embrace the snow days that come our way. Go ahead, bundle up and get outside, or curl up with a good book. Slow down and enjoy the moment. Soak up the unique wonder that only a snow day can bring. For I hope you always remember, it's these unexpected breaks from routine that make life so special.

I HOPE YOU HAVE LEARNED

There Is Always Someone, Smarter Than You

It's a humbling realization, but an important one: no matter how much you know, no matter how intelligent you may be, there is always someone smarter than you. This fact can be both daunting and liberating. Daunting, because it's a reminder that there will always be others who surpass you in knowledge and ability. Liberating, because it frees you from the need to be the smartest person in the room. So you're *not* the smartest person in the world. And guess what? That's okay!

Here's the thing about life (and school, and work, and everything in between): you'll always meet someone who's got more knowledge, more experience, or some secret trivia about penguins that somehow makes them sound smarter than you in a room full of people. It can feel like you're always playing catch-up, but here's why that's actually a good thing. There is always going to be someone smarter (or better, faster, or more talented). And guess what? That's what makes life interesting. If you were the smartest in every room, wouldn't you eventually get bored? Instead, being around people who excel at different things is a gift! It's how you grow. That person who's got a photographic memory or writes essays with the speed of light? They're a reminder that there's always something new you can learn. Bonus points if you actually ask them something instead of comparing yourself to them.

Being "the smartest in the room" isn't the goal, and it never has been. Instead of focusing on how much you know, shift your energy to **what you can learn**. Surrounding yourself with people who challenge you is one of the fastest ways to grow—not just academically, but as a person. When you're around people who are "smarter," you get access to their ideas, perspectives, and solutions. That's an opportunity, not competition.

Here's a little perspective check for when you start spiraling into comparison mode (we've all been there):

- The person you think is smart? They've felt clueless before, too. Probably recently.
- You bring something unique to the table, even if it's not a Nobel Prize-level brain. Maybe it's creativity. Maybe you make legendary grilled cheese sandwiches. The point is, brilliance comes in different forms.
- Collaboration beats competition. Every time.

You don't have to know everything. Learning doesn't stop when you leave high school or college; it's a lifelong process. No one has it all figured out, even if they look super confident while using 17-syllable words in conversation. Being smart is cool, sure. But being curious? That's unstoppable. If you're open to growth, willing to listen, and comfortable stepping outside your comfort zone, you'll always surprise yourself with how much you can achieve.

Recognizing that there is always someone smarter than you opens you up to a lifetime of learning. When you accept that you don't have all the answers, that there is always more to discover, you cultivate a growth mindset. You become curious, hungry for new knowledge and experiences. You seek out others who can teach you, who can share their expertise and insights. However the idea that there is always someone smarter than you isn't just about individual growth. It's also a reminder of the power of collaboration and community. When you acknowledge that others have knowledge and skills you lack, you're able to work together towards common goals. You learn to value diverse perspectives, to appreciate the unique contributions each person can make. This recognition that we're all smarter together than we are alone is key to achieving great things. Feeling inadequate because someone seems smarter, faster, or more talented? Remember, it's not a competition—it's a community. Life isn't about being the smartest in the room; it's about learning and growing.

Surround yourself with people who challenge and inspire you. Being humble enough to admit you don't know everything opens the door to wisdom and deeper connections. Celebrate the strengths of others and focus on your unique gifts. You have a purpose, and comparing yourself to others only distracts you from fulfilling it. Lean into collaboration, not comparison, and trust in the beauty of your individual journey.

Advice From Someone That Loves You:

I kinda doubt this is true because I think you are the smartest person alive but I guess there is always someone smarter. No matter what we do, we find that there is always someone that is better at it than we are. Even star olympic athletes often get shocked by someone. I hope you seek out those who can teach you, who can challenge your thinking and push you to grow. I hope you cultivate a love of learning that lasts a lifetime. And always remember, true wisdom lies not in knowing everything, but in recognizing how much you have yet to learn. There will always be someone smarter than you. But no one else on this planet has your perspective, personality, or potential. That's your edge. Own it.

I HOPE YOU HAVE LEARNED

Pets Don't Live Forever

Somethings are more permanent than others. It's never easy. You come home to an empty house after years of wagging tails, purring snuggles, or that one curious fish who always seemed oddly aware of your presence. Losing a pet feels heavier than words can describe because they were family. No questions asked, just unconditional love wrapped in fur, scales, or feathers.

For many, this state of loss may even feel out of place or overwhelming, especially at a time when your life is already full of transition. Maybe you've just graduated, moved away from home, or started your first real "adulting" job. Life is tossing you curveballs, and on top of it all, you're reminded that even your pets aren't permanent.

While there's no magical fix that makes the grief disappear, it's okay to feel the loss deeply. They weren't "just a dog," "just a cat," or "just a hamster." They were the beacon of comfort, the ones who didn't care if you aced that exam or bombed it, who cheered you on with slobbery kisses or quiet companionship after tough times with friends or family. But even in this loss, there's something beautiful to hold onto. Pets teach us a lot about life (without them even realizing they're doing it). They teach us to:

- **Live in the Moment** - Ever notice how a dog chases sticks with the same excitement for the 500th time? It's a reminder to be present, to cherish now.
- **Love Without Conditions** - Pets don't judge. A good cuddle or a boop on the nose reminds us love is simple and can come without strings attached.
- **Find Joy in Small Things** - Whether it was a cardboard box, a sunbeam to nap in, or the crinkle of a treat bag, they found joy in simplicity. You can, too.

Even as you grieve, hold onto their lessons. Reflect on the moments they made you laugh, the warmth they brought when you felt like no one else understood, and the ridiculous antics that gave life color. For young adults who might be figuring life out (or at least pretending to), it's tough to hear this, but pets are another way life gently reminds us that things change and the world moves forward, whether we're prepared for it or not. That doesn't mean letting go of memories. It means celebrating what they left behind in your life.

Maybe, one day, when you're ready, another set of paws, wings, or fins will find their way into your world. But for now, it's okay to hold your favorite mug of coffee or tea, stare at their favorite napping spot, and thank them for being the simple, loyal friends you never knew you needed so much. And hey, don't forget to laugh. Remember the time they tripped over their own feet? Or when they managed to chew something into oblivion and look proud about it? Yeah, them. What a gift.

Pets allow us to truly appreciate how temporary the time that we have with them is. It encourages us to cherish each moment, to give them the best life possible and to not take any day for granted. It motivates us to provide them with a happy and healthy home, to give them all the love and care they deserve. And it reminds us to be present, to put away our phones and simply enjoy the time we have with our companions. But even with this mindset, the loss of a pet is devastating. The bond we form with our animals is deep and profound, built on years of shared experiences and unconditional love. They are more than just pets, they are members of our family and dear friends. And when they're gone, the pain can be overwhelming. Grieving the loss of a pet is a process, one that looks different for everyone. There's no right or wrong way to grieve, just the need to allow ourselves to feel the pain of our loss. And as the days turn into weeks, and the weeks into months, the pain begins to lessen. We start to remember more of the good times, of the joy and love our pets brought into our lives. We realize that the pain of loss is a testament to the depth of our bond, and that it was all worth it for the time we had together. And eventually, we may even find ourselves ready to open our hearts and homes to another furry friend in need. Pets remind us to cherish life's moments, but their time is finite. Love deeply, knowing God's eternal love never fades.

Advice From Someone That Loves You:

We know our pets, although very special, are not permanent but I hope you have a pet at some time in your life that you love. If you're thinking of getting a pet, and it is the right time, do it. Yes, the impermanence of their lives can be painful, but the joy and love they bring is well worth it. Cherish each moment, provide them with the best life possible, and don't be afraid to show them love. Because in the end, it's not the grief of loss we should fear, but the regret of never having experienced the incredible bond of human and animal.

I HOPE YOU HAVE LEARNED

Making Mistakes Are Expected

Growing up is a journey of discovery. It's a time of learning, exploring, and figuring out who we are and where we fit in the world. And an inevitable part of this journey is making mistakes. You Messed Up? Welcome to the Club. Here's the thing about making mistakes: we all do it. Whether you forgot a friend's birthday, completely bombed that chemistry exam, or sent an email to "Professor Smith" that started with "Hey pal" (ouch), mistakes happen. They're as much a part of life as Wi-Fi issues during a Zoom meeting. Yet when you make a mistake, it's easy to spiral. "Why did I do that?" you may ask yourself, replaying the moment over and over like it's an embarrassing scene in a high-stakes soap opera. But guess what? Nobody's life script goes perfectly.

One of the biggest myths is that every mistake is a roadblock. Nope. Think of mistakes as speed bumps. Sure, they can slow you down, but they're not worth stopping for too long. Overthinking them doesn't undo them, but what does help is to ask yourself, "What can I learn from this?" You didn't study for that test? Now you know to plan better. Hurt someone's feelings? Now you know how to communicate more thoughtfully next time. Signed up for too many extracurriculars and find yourself buried? Hey, now you know your limits. Mistakes are like tiny (sometimes huge) life tutors, teaching things you didn't know you needed.

Serious mistakes aside, some goof-ups are just plain funny when you think about them. Like spilling your coffee and dropping a textbook in front of everyone on the same day. Embarrassing? Sure. But are people going to be replaying your spills in their heads for years? Absolutely not. Most of the time, people are thinking about their own "oh no" moments, not yours. Laugh at yourself. It's freeing and way better than stressing over perfection.

Years from now, you'll probably look back and chuckle at some of the things stressing you out now. That thing that seems absolutely life-ending today? You barely remembers it. Life is long, and one (or even ten) mistakes can't stop you in your tracks. Here's the bottom line. You're human, and humans are wired to make mistakes. Instead of beating yourself up, take the moment to learn, grow, and keep moving forward. You've got a huge adventure ahead, and trust me, a stumble here or there only makes the story that much more interesting.

Now, go handle today or tomorrow knowing you're going to crush it—with or without the occasional stumble.

As children, we learn by doing. We stumble, we fall and we try again. We touch the hot stove and learn it burns. We color on the wall and learn it's not a canvas. These early mistakes teach us boundaries, rules, and consequences. They help shape our understanding of the world and guide our actions. As we get older, our mistakes become more complex. We might say something mean to a friend and we learning about the power of words. We may take a risk that doesn't pay off, teaching us about failure and resilience. Or we might make a choice that has bigger consequences, like getting in trouble at school or damaging a relationship. These mistakes can be painful, but they offer valuable lessons about responsibility, decision-making, and integrity. Making mistakes is how we learn and grow. It's through error and failure that we gain wisdom and insight.

Thomas Edison, when inventing the light bulb, said, I have not failed. I've just found 10,000 ways that won't work. Mistakes are not setbacks, but steps on the path to success. In today's world, there can be a pressure to be perfect. Social media showcases the highlights of other people's lives, making it seem like everyone else has it together. There's an emphasis on achievement, on getting good grades, playing sports, volunteering, and building a perfect college application. And in this atmosphere, mistakes can feel catastrophic. So instead of fearing mistakes, we should embrace them as opportunities for growth. When we mess up, instead of beating ourselves up over it, we should reflect on what went wrong and how we can do better next time.

Advice From Someone That Loves You:

I wish I could tell you how many mistakes I made in my life. I made some mistakes that I honestly hope you never find out about because they were embarrassing. Just like me, you will mess up, and when you do, I hope you practice self-compassion. Please remind yourself that everyone makes mistakes, and that it's okay not to be perfect. Let's learn what we can from the experience, pick ourselves up, and keep moving forward. Because that's the only way to truly grow, and to become the person we're meant to be. Here's a little secret no one tells you about adulthood (or life in general): Nobody has it all figured out. That professor who seems to know everything? They've probably mispronounced "quinoa" at some point. That "perfect" student crushing it on Instagram? They've definitely used salt instead of sugar in a recipe. You're not alone. You're not broken. You're just growing. Mistakes don't define you; how you respond to them does.

I HOPE YOU HAVE LEARNED

Failing Is The Beginning, Not The End

Success is often held up as the ultimate goal. We strive to win, to achieve, to accomplish. We set targets, make plans, and work hard to reach them. And when we hit our marks, when we succeed, it feels amazing. But while success is sweet, failure can be a far more powerful teacher.

Ever feel like failure has the biggest spotlight on you? Whether it's failing a test, not getting into your dream college, or royally messing up a big project, failure can feel like the end of the road. Cue the dramatic background music and black-and-white slow-mo scene of you staring out the window. But honestly? Failing isn't the big bad wolf out to ruin your life. It's often just the plot twist in the story you didn't see coming. Here's the truth that nobody really tells us in high school or college classes: failure is normal. Like, super normal. Life is a giant trial-and-error experiment, and while we all hope to nail things on the first try, the reality is that sometimes you're going to mess up. That's part of the process. (Spoiler alert: adults are just bigger kids still figuring this out.)

If you're never failing, you're not really trying things that stretch you. Success can teach us something, sure. But failure? It screams, "Hey! You're stepping outside of your comfort zone!" That C+ you got on a chemistry final wasn't the end; it was proof you're learning. (Also, balance equations are a scam, right?) Failing is basically nature's brutally honest teacher. Didn't land that internship? Maybe the rejection gets you to rework your resume or think harder about what really excites you. Flopped at leading a group project? Now you know not to choose Todd as a partner again.

Failing Means You're in Good Company. Guess who's failed big time?

- Oprah? Yep, she was told she was "unfit for TV."
- Michael Jordan? Kicked off his high school basketball team.
- J.K. Rowling? Rejected by over 12 publishers for a little story called Harry Potter.
- Failures are practically a membership card to the success club.

When failure happens (not if, *when*), ask yourself this:

- What Can I Learn? Rewrite the script in your head from "I failed" to "What did this teach me?"
- Where Can I Pivot? Sometimes failure nudges us toward opportunities we wouldn't have otherwise considered.
- Didn't get the job? Maybe it's because the right one is still waiting for you.
- How Do I Keep Going? Taking that next baby step might feel impossible, but momentum is everything. One positive action can change the whole vibe.

When we fail, when we fall short, when things don't go as planned, it can be tough to take. We might feel defeated, demoralized, and doubtful of ourselves. But if we can push through the initial sting of failure, if we can reflect and learn, we can gain insights and grow in ways success alone cannot provide. Failure teaches us resilience. When we fail, we have two choices: we can give up, or we can get back up and try again. And it's in getting back up, in persisting despite setbacks, that we build strength and tenacity. Failure provides feedback. When we succeed, it can be hard to know what worked and what we can improve. But failure gives us clear signals. We can look at what went wrong, where we fell short, and use that to refine our approach. Failure fosters creativity. When our initial plans don't work out, we're forced to think differently. We have to come up with new solutions, try different approaches, and innovate. And it's in this process of problem-solving that we can discover novel ideas and grow as thinkers. Failure builds humility. Success can make us feel invincible, like we have all the answers. But failure brings us back down to earth. It reminds us that we're not perfect, that we can always improve. And it's in this place of humility that we can learn and grow. Failure is not the opposite of success, but a part of it. The most successful people have also failed the most. J.K. Rowling was a single mom living on welfare when twelve publishers rejected Harry Potter. Stephen King's first novel, Carrie, was rejected thirty times. And Henry Ford went bankrupt twice before the Ford Motor Company succeeded. Failure is not a roadblock to success, but a stepping stone.

Advice From Someone That Loves You:

I know you will fail, and it may sound hard, but I'm glad that you already have and know how it feels. I hope you remember that everyone fails, and that it's okay not to be perfect. I hope you learn what you can from the experience, pick yourself up, and keep moving forward. Because you are destined to greatness. Often failure signals the start of something great. It is only a dead-end for a bad idea. Embrace your failures and let them lead you to your next success. I am counting on that. Failing isn't fun, but it's not final. It's messy and humbling, but it's also where the best stories and the biggest personal growth happen. You will fail at some point. But guess what? You'll survive. And more importantly, you'll thrive. Every beginning starts somewhere —even if it starts with a fail.

I HOPE YOU HAVE LEARNED

How It Feels To Be Part Of A Team

Some of the most meaningful and impactful achievements come not from working alone, but from working as part of a team. When you think of being part of a team, what's the first thing that pops into your mind? Whether it's the camaraderie of winning a volleyball championship, late nights spent working on a group project, or, let's be honest, that one person who swore they'd "get their part done" but vanished, being part of a team comes with its unique set of feelings and experiences. And here's the thing about teams, whether they're on the court, in class, or built during your first job interview prep with friends—they leave a mark on you. A good team can build you up, teach you things about yourself, and make tough challenges feel a little less daunting.

At its best, being in a team makes you feel like you belong. You're seen, your ideas matter, and you're contributing to something bigger than yourself. It's high-fives after a win, belly laughs over shared inside jokes, and that satisfying *click* when everyone's efforts come together. But, let's keep it real—not all team experiences are golden. Sometimes, deadlines loom, group chat messages are "seen" but ignored, and everyone's just this close to losing it.

Teamwork can be messy and imperfect, but it's in those moments that you figure out a lot about who you are. Can you take a deep breath and lead? Are you willing to step back and listen when it's needed? It's all part of the package.

Here's a little secret they don't always tell you in leadership conferences and cheesy motivational posters. Being in a team doesn't automatically make everything easier. However, working together teaches you resilience, empathy, and the art of showing up.

- **You learn to celebrate others:** Success feels so much sweeter when it's shared. High-five the friend who nailed their presentation or passed their idea in the group meeting that saved everyone's grade.
- **You build thicker skin:** Working through disagreements? Tough, but it teaches you how to collaborate respectfully.
- **You find people who get you**: Teams are where life-long friendships are formed. Guaranteed, five years from now, you may not remember every detail of that project, but you'll remember how you made each other feel.

There's power in knowing you don't have to go it alone. Whether you're huddled over study notes with friends or putting on your freshman-year jersey, there's something incredible about leaning into that connection.

You might be the ideas person, the peacemaker, the last-minute inventor (aka, crunch-time hero), or the quiet observer who swoops in with *just* the right suggestion at the right time. Whatever your style, every role matters. Your contributions help the bigger picture come to life. And guess what? You don't have to be perfect. Teams aren't about the spotlight; they're about shared effort. Show up and try—that's more than enough.

Being part of a team is a lot like life itself. It's chaotic, inspiring, frustrating, creative, and full of opportunities to grow. Whether you're studying for finals or tackling a new "real-world" job, remember this: the best teams aren't flawless, but they show up for each other. Sure, you might end up venting to your roommate every now and then about who didn't pull their weight, but hey—that's all part of the experience too, right? Whether you're leading, following, or hyping up your team from the sidelines, know this...you're making an impact. Now, go out there and be the teammate someone else remembers in the best way years down the line.

When we collaborate with others, when we pool our skills and strengths, we can accomplish far more than we ever could on our own. And when we win as a team, when our collective efforts lead to success, it's a unique and powerful kind of victory. Competing with a team requires a different mindset than competing as an individual. When we're on our own, it's all about our own performance. We focus on our goals, our progress, and our results. But when we're part of a team, we have to think about more than just ourselves. We have to consider our teammates, our roles, and how we can work together most effectively. Trust is essential for a team to succeed. When you're working with others, you have to know that they've got your back. You have to trust that they'll do their part, that they'll be reliable and committed. And you have to earn their trust in return by following through on your commitments and being there for them. When a team is working well together, it's a powerful thing. You can feel the energy and momentum. Ideas flow, progress happens, and you can achieve far more than you would on your own. And when you win as a team, when your collective efforts lead to success, it's an incredible feeling. But even more importantly, competing with a team teaches you valuable skills that you can apply to all areas of your life. You learn how to communicate, how to delegate, and how to work through challenges as part of a group. You learn how to lead and how to follow, how to give feedback and how to receive it. And you learn how to trust in yourself and in others.

Advice From Someone That Loves You:

Do you remember participating on a team when you were little. It may have been a terrible experience or it may have been a great one, but one thing I am sure of, you will remember it. I hope you continue to get the chance to compete with a team regardless of your age. Put yourself out there, figure out your role, and go all in. It won't always be easy – there will be challenges and disagreements along the way. But if you learn how to stick together, if you can communicate and trust in each other, there's no limit to what you can achieve. This is a lesson you will use over and over.

I HOPE YOU HAVE LEARNED

To Make Time To Pick Up Seashells

One of the simplest yet most profound joys in life is collecting shells on the beach. It's an activity that connects us to nature, sparks our curiosity, and brings us peace. When we walk along the shore, eyes scanning the sand, we become like kids again, full of wonder and awe. The first thing you notice when you start collecting shells is the incredible variety. There are so many different types, each with its own unique shape, size, and color. Some are delicate and translucent, others are big and bold. Some have intricate patterns, others are smooth and plain. And every now and then, you'll find a truly special one, a shell that stands out from the rest. As you search for shells, you start to notice the little things. The way the light catches a fragment of glass, the sound of the waves crashing against the shore, the feel of the sand beneath your feet. You become present in the moment, fully engaged with your surroundings. It's a form of meditation, a way to quiet the mind and tune into the world around you.

Life has a way of moving fast. If you're a college student or a recent high school graduate, you probably already feel the pressure to figure everything out. Courses to take, careers to pursue, decisions to make. It's as if we all got handed a checklist with no pause button. But amidst the chaos, here's a little reminder for you: don't forget to pick up the seashells. Now, I'm not just talking about seashells literally (although if you live near a beach, go for it!). I'm talking about those little moments that might seem inconsequential but are actually the treasures of life. Watching the sunset. Grabbing late-night ice cream with friends. Laughing so hard you forget what started it. Or maybe it's sitting quietly by yourself, enjoying a cup of coffee without a single notification intruding. These "seashell moments" are the things you'll remember. Not how you crammed for that Tuesday test or stressed over a class group project. It's important to work hard, study smarter, and build your future —but it's equally important to realize that life's best moments aren't found one day in the distant future when your "checklist" is blank. They're sprinkled in your ordinary days, waiting to be noticed. Imagine going to the beach for hours, only to realize you were so busy running back and forth that you didn't look down to pick up a single seashell. That's what life can feel like if you don't pause every now and then.

What Can You Do Today to Pick Up a Seashell?

- Take a Mental Break: Even if it's just 10 minutes. Step away from your textbooks or that internship application and just breathe in a little quiet.
- Share a Laugh with Someone: Call a friend, tell them their last meme post was terrible, and watch the conversation unravel into five different topics.

- Notice Small Joys: The world is full of them. That first sip of coffee, the warmth of sunlight sneaking through your curtains, or even just catching a great parking spot on campus.
- Say Yes to Something Fun: We get it, responsibility is important, but so is spontaneity. Go karaoke horribly. Try that weird sushi roll someone dared you to.

It's okay to keep your GPA up. It's okay to hustle for the dream career. What's not okay is forgetting that life isn't just the huge goals. It's also all the tiny moments you collect in between. College and early adulthood are hard enough without racing through it all. Don't rob yourself of the simple, silly, and sometimes magical "seashells" hidden in plain sight. Because, sure, you could be productive every single second. Or you could live a little. Heads-up, I hear the best seashells aren't always the prettiest. Sometimes, they're the ones with cracks and jagged edges, but they've got the best stories to tell. That's the stuff worth picking up.

Collecting shells is also a way to slow down and appreciate the small things. In our fast-paced world, we often rush from one thing to the next, never stopping to smell the roses. But when we're searching for shells, we have to move at a different pace. We have to be patient, to take our time, to really look. And in doing so, we find joy in the journey, not just the destination. Cherish small moments. Life's scattered blessings often resemble seashells on the shore—beautiful, unique, and easily overlooked.

Advice From Someone That Loves You:

The shells are all broken, scattered and hurt your feet.
However, try to image their journey to where you are finding
them. It has been very tough I imagine. So next time you're at
the beach, take a walk along the shore. Keep your eyes peeled
for that special shell. See what the ocean has washed up, what
treasures it has brought just to you. And as you walk,
remember to be present. Notice the feel of the sand, the sound
of the waves, the smell of the salt air. Notice the way the light
catches the water, the way the breeze rustles your hair. Be
fully in the moment, fully engaged with the world around
you.

I HOPE YOU HAVE LEARNED

How It Feels When You Fall Off A Bike

Falling off a bike is a rite of passage for many of us. Falling off a bike is a pretty universal experience. One minute, you're cruising along, feeling like you've got it all figured out, and the next, you're face down on the pavement, wondering what just happened. It's messy. It's embarrassing. And honestly? It hurts. Life is kind of like riding a bike. Whether you're tackling a college schedule stuffed with 8 a.m. classes or figuring out your post-graduation plans, there are going to be moments that feel like wiping out on gravel.

When you fall, the first thing you feel isn't the pain. It's shock. You sit there for a second, stunned, wondering, How did this even happen? Maybe someone distracted you. Maybe you hit an unexpected bump in the road. Or maybe you just lost focus. Whatever the cause, you didn't plan on being here —in this awkward, bruised, less-than-glamorous moment. Life's the same. Sometimes we hit the ground because we failed. Maybe that exam didn't go as planned or the internship fell through. Other times, it's because of something completely out of our control. Either way, the ground is the same, and getting up feels impossible for a moment. Then there's the sting. Whether it's a scraped knee or a bruised ego, the pain makes itself known. It's easy to replay the fall in your head and think, I should've seen this coming. You beat yourself up for not being perfect, not anticipating every rock in the road, every unexpected turn. But here's the thing about pain: it's a sign you're human. Falling doesn't mean you're a bad cyclist (or a bad student, or a bad friend, or fill-in-the-blank). It just means you're learning. Every sharp edge teaches you to adjust, to lean into the curve, to find your balance again.

Eventually, you get up. Maybe you dust yourself off. Maybe you limp a little. Maybe there's a wobble in your first few pedals. The thing is, you don't stay down. Because staying there, face down on the pavement, isn't the end of your story. Getting back on the bike feels scary at first, but once you start moving, confidence catches on. Remember this if nothing else: falling doesn't mean you've failed long-term. It's a reminder you dared to take the ride in the first place. The wobble, the bruise, the scab on your knee—that's proof of your effort, not evidence of your defeat.

Here's the truth hidden behind every fall, every mistake, every "what even just happened" moment you face. It's not about the fall; it's about how you rise. Each stumble makes you stronger, tougher, and just a little wiser. And who knows? The stronger you get, the more daring your rides might become. Whether it's navigating job rejections, adapting to a new city, or just finding balance when everything feels overwhelming, know this—every time you fall, you're learning something that makes the next ride smoother. Now go find your balance, college warrior. Every scrape teaches, every bruise heals, and every fall pushes you toward the next big ride.

Falling off a bike is jarring, isn't it? One moment, you're confidently pedaling along, the wind rushing past you, feeling unstoppable. The next? You're on the ground, scraped up, bruised, and stunned. Life has a way of feeling like that sometimes. One moment, everything seems to be moving along just as it should—and then, out of nowhere, the fall happens. Maybe it's a failed exam, a broken relationship, or a setback in a project you poured your heart into. Suddenly, you're not sure how to get back up, and the bruises feel too painful to touch. But here's the thing about falling off a bike —you get to pick yourself up. The process might be messy, and you might be hesitant to climb back on, but you have the courage and determination to give it another shot. It's the same with life. Falling teaches us more than we expect—it humbles, strengthens, and sharpens us. Even in moments when getting up feels impossible, remember this: you are surrounded by the tools and people that can help.

Lean on friends, mentors, or your faith when the bruises feel too raw. Give yourself grace to heal, and don't rush the process. Most of all, trust that each "fall" is shaping you for bigger and better rides ahead. Whether you're coasting downhill or climbing the steepest hill, falls don't define us—how we rise does. Today, reflect on how you've risen before, and know you have that same strength within you right now. The bike's waiting. When you're ready, climb back on.

.

Advice From Someone That Loves You:

I know that you remember falling off your bike and that it was not fun, but it was not the end of the world either. Often it is more embarrassing than painful. You may have acted like it hurt to save face, but aren't you glad you remember how that felt. Many times even the things we do all the time fail to go as expected. There will be many simple tasks that you know well how to do, that you will fail at. But when you do, with a few deep breaths, and some determination, you'll be back in the saddle in no time. Don't quit!

I HOPE YOU HAVE LEARNED

Some People Get Sick, And They Don't Get Well

Life isn't always simple or fair. One of the hardest realities we face is accepting that some people get sick and don't get better. It's a question many of us wrestle with, especially when it feels like there's no clear reason for the suffering. Life isn't a straight road. It's more like a series of plot twists written by a writer who loves cliffhangers. Sometimes, those twists include sickness, and, for some people, healing doesn't come this side of the story. It's a reality we don't like to talk about, especially when you're young and just stepping into "adulthood" (whatever that means). After all, you're supposed to be invincible in your prime, aren't you? But the truth is, sometimes people face illnesses that don't simply go away.

Here's something to think about: it's okay not to have all the answers. You're not a flawed person if you don't understand why someone gets sick and doesn't recover. You're human. Some questions stay unanswered no matter how many mental Google searches you run. And honestly? That's frustrating. But in the pause between asking and understanding, there's room to grow. Maybe it teaches us compassion. Maybe it's a nudge to hold the people around us a little closer.

If someone you care about is sick and their health isn't improving, you don't have to know magical words to make things better. Just be there. Sometimes people don't need your wisdom; they just need your presence.

- **How to Show Up:** Text a meme to brighten their day. Visit when you can, and don't worry if your visits include awkward silences. Awkward silences are strangely comforting sometimes.
- **How to Listen:** If they want to talk about the hard stuff, lean in and listen. If they don't, that's okay too. Follow their lead.
- **How to Celebrate Small Wins:** Got to the mailbox today? Awesome! Watched three episodes of a Netflix series instead of one? That's binge-watching talent! Celebrate every inch of progress, no matter how insignificant it may seem to the rest of the world.

If you're the one watching someone you love go through this, you might feel drained or helpless. Remember to take care of your own mental health, too. It's not selfish; it's necessary. Here's the thing to always remember, though. Life can throw a lot at you, but whether you're the sick one or the friend watching from the sidelines, it's not about being perfect. It's about trying, showing up, and loving as hard as you can. And honestly, even in the depths of difficulty, there's something beautiful in that.

Illness touches not only the individual but everyone who loves them, making us wonder why healing doesn't always come the way we hope. If you've lost someone, or you're watching someone you care about struggle with their health, it's completely natural to feel a mix of emotions— sadness, frustration, and maybe even anger. These feelings don't make you weak or wrong; they make you human. But when you feel overwhelmed, remember this — it's okay not to have all the answers. Some things are beyond our understanding, but they're not outside of God's presence.

Even in the darkest circumstances, we can trust that God sees, knows, and walks with us through the uncertainty. It doesn't mean the pain will disappear, but it means we don't have to carry it alone. What can we do when healing doesn't come? Start by loving fiercely. Be present for those who are hurting. Sometimes, the most healing thing we can offer is simply being there—a hand to hold, a shoulder to cry on, a prayer whispered in quiet moments. And as you walk through this, hold on to hope. Hope that even when we don't understand, the story isn't over. Hope that love, faith, and community can offer comfort in the face of loss. If you're struggling today, know this—you're not alone. You are surrounded by a God who loves you deeply and a community that cares for you. Lean into that love. And if you need a little extra strength, say a simple prayer for peace and guidance in the moments ahead. Look, life isn't always tied up in a neat bow. For some folks, the reality of "getting better" might not be on the table. And while that's heavy, it's not the only story. People are more than what happens to them. There's beauty in the resilience and humor that show up in the middle of the mess. To the friend who feels helpless supporting someone sick, remember this one thing: your presence is powerful. And to the one who's struggling? It's okay to rest. You're pretty awesome just as you are. Now, go grab a coffee or send that text you've been meaning to. Little things matter. You matter.

Advice From Someone That Loves You:

Sometimes people we love get sick and they get well. However, sometimes people get sick and they don't. It feels unfair many times as we don't understand why that happens to some and not to others. I know you will or have experienced this, How much we want people that we love to get well. How much we want our lives to just go back to the way they were. But the reality is our life on this earth is not all there is, and we are just passing through. So remember, death is not the end, it is the beginning.

I HOPE YOU HAVE LEARNED

Tomorrow Is Not Guaranteed

The statement tomorrow is not promised transcends cultures and generations. It serves as a stark reminder of the inherent uncertainty and preciousness of life. When you're young, there's this unwritten confidence that tomorrow will always be there. You plan, you dream, you procrastinate (a lot), and you think, "I'll get to it tomorrow." Sounds familiar, right? Whether it's studying for a big test, calling a friend back, or finally launching that side hustle that's been sitting in the back of your brain, it's easy to assume that there's always going to be more time. But here's a real talk moment for you—life doesn't send out save-the-dates. We can't control what happens tomorrow, but we can control what we do with today.

Still holding onto that apology you know you owe someone? Make it. Been too scared to try because failing feels worse than not starting at all? Try, even if you stumble on the way. Have something you've been dying to say to someone who means the world to you? Say it. Don't bank on "later" being your fallback plan. Because here's the truth—not everything can (or should) be put on your "someday" calendar.

But I get it; doing "all the things" can be overwhelming. You're running on coffee, stress, and vibes most of the time. No one's expecting you to have life all figured out in one afternoon. Not even close. The trick is to focus on the small yet meaningful steps you can take today. Here are a few ideas to get you started:

- **Write It Down**: Whether it's a to-do list or a single goal, putting things on paper makes them feel tangible. Plus, there's something satisfying about crossing things off.
- **Reach Out**: Send that text, make that call, or drop that note. Just connect. Relationships deserve your time, and sometimes it only takes a simple "I'm thinking of you" to show someone they matter.
- **Learn Something New**: Read a few pages of a book, research a topic that sparks your curiosity, or watch a video tutorial on that one thing you swore you'd learn but haven't yet.
- **Take a Leap**: That thing you've been avoiding? Face it head-on. Just starting is often the hardest part, but it's also where growth begins.
- **Rest on Purpose**: Not everything has to be about productivity. If today means prioritizing rest, do it unapologetically. Balance is key.

The beauty of living in this moment is that it doesn't need to be groundbreaking to be meaningful. Maybe your "today" looks like grabbing coffee with an old friend or finally cleaning out that drawer that's become a black hole of random cables. Or maybe it's simply sitting down, reflecting, and deciding that you're enough as you are right now. Tomorrow might not be guaranteed, but today is. Make it count.

Every day we wake up, every breath we take, is a gift – and yet, we often take for granted that tomorrow will inevitably come. This phrase shakes us out of that complacency, forcing us to confront the reality that the future is never guaranteed. It's a call to live in the present, to prioritize what truly adds meaning and value to our lives, and to pursue our dreams and aspirations with urgency and intention. When we internalize the truth that tomorrow is not promised, it shifts our perspective. We begin to see each day as an opportunity, rather than an obligation. We're compelled to let go of petty grudges, to speak our truth, and to express love and appreciation to those around us.

Rather than putting off until tomorrow what we can do today, we're inspired to take action, to seize the moment, and to make the most of the time we have. It's a reminder that regret can be a heavy burden, and that the greatest regrets are often the chances we don't take and the words we leave unspoken. Tomorrow is not guaranteed, and every moment is a gift. Life is full of unexpected turns, reminding us to cherish today and live purposefully. Seek wisdom, love deeply, and invest in what truly matters. Don't put off what's in your heart for another day—take action now to grow, forgive, and connect. By living fully in the present, you honor the life

you've been given and reflect grace to those around you.
Make today count.

Advice From Someone That Loves You:

You have a lot of things you have to do. You may even be planning on doing some of them tomorrow. But what if tomorrow doesn't come. I want you to live in a way that honors the present. It's about treating each day as a precious gift, and making the most of the time you have. It's about living with intention, with gratitude, and with a deep appreciation for the beauty and fragility of life itself. When we embrace this truth, we open ourselves up to a more authentic, more meaningful, and more fulfilling existence. I want you to learn to cherish every moment, to pursue your dreams with passion, and to leave a lasting legacy.

I HOPE YOU HAVE LEARNED

Everything, Is Not About You

The statement everything is not about you is a powerful reminder that has the potential to shift our perspective and improve our interactions with others. Here's some real talk for you. Somewhere along the way, life can start to feel like a big, dramatic movie, with you cast as the lead character. The spotlight's on YOU. Every class, every relationship, every follower on Instagram, every like, every text that gets left on "read"… it all feels personal. But here comes the plot twist (cue suspenseful music): it's not all about you. Now, don't roll your eyes just yet. There's freedom in this idea! When you're not the center of the universe (spoiler alert, you're not), the world becomes much bigger, more complex, and honestly more exciting.

If you're walking out of high school or entering college, guess what? You're stepping into a life stage where everything feels like a competition. People worry about their grades, their careers, or their place in the friend group. It's easy to get caught in the spiral of "What does this mean for me?" But when you take a step back, you'll start to see that people aren't circling around your orbit (and that's totally okay). Most people are just trying to deal with their own stuff, not plotting how to ruin your day. You forgot to say something cool during that group meeting? Nobody noticed. You waved at someone, and they didn't wave back? They probably didn't even see you. It's not about not caring or ignoring yourself. It's about getting OUTSIDE your head and seeing what you might miss when your world stops revolving around, well, you.

- **You stress less:** If not everything is about YOU, then not every challenge is about YOUR failure. Sometimes stuff just happens, and it has nothing to do with you at all. That's a relief, right?

- **You connect better:** When you stop worrying whether people are judging you or thinking about you, you actually start to listen to them. You care more honestly and deeply. Relationships grow stronger when you're not just waiting for your turn to talk.

- **You show up differently:** When you're not the "star," you can be the supporting character in someone else's story. And here's the cool bit—that's not a downgrade. Supporting characters often bring the most joy and unexpected value to the plot.

Here's a little perspective check for you. Look up at the sky tonight. You see those millions of stars? Somewhere out there, entire galaxies are spinning around, and they couldn't care less whether you wore jeans or sweatpants to class today. Wild, right? Or think about coffee. That barista didn't misspell your name on purpose. They weren't plotting to ruin your morning. They've taken 87 orders before you even walked up, and half their brain is wondering if they'll pass their biology exam tonight. It's nothing personal.

Here's the key takeaway. Realizing that everything's not about you doesn't minimize your value or worth. You are important—but not more important than everyone else. And that's not a bad thing. It's an invitation to be part of something bigger, something that doesn't just depend on YOU. The world is a shared stage, and you're playing alongside countless other people with their own dreams, struggles, and joys. When you stop trying to make it all about you, you'll notice so much more going on. And guess what? That's where the good stuff lives.

Shift your perspective today. During conversations or interactions, try asking yourself, "What's THEIR story?" Instead of making an assumption or reacting emotionally, focus on what the person in front of you might be experiencing. Practice seeing beyond your own movie script. It's scary (and humbling) to realize you're not the center of the universe, but once you do, you'll start seeing just how vibrant and connected the world can be. It's so much better when we're all in this together.…and yes, you're allowed to keep being awesome. Just remember, everyone else is too.

In a world where we're often encouraged to focus on ourselves, this idea may seem counterintuitive. However, understanding that everything is not about us can be incredibly liberating. At its core, this means that other people's actions, reactions, and emotions are frequently a reflection of their own thoughts, experiences, and struggles. When someone snaps at us, forgets a commitment, or seems distant, our initial reaction might be to take it personally. We may wonder what we did wrong or how we can fix the situation. But the truth is, much of the time, other people's behavior has little to do with us and a lot to do with what they're going through. Are they going through a tough time at work or in their personal life? Are they struggling with stress, anxiety, or other emotions that have nothing to do with us? By taking a step back and considering these factors, we can respond in a more compassionate and patient way. *Everything is not about you* also promotes healthier relationships. When we stop taking everything so personally, we create space for more open and honest communication. We're less likely to jump to conclusions or react impulsively out of fear or insecurity. Instead, we can address issues in a calm and constructive manner, which can lead to greater understanding and closeness. In addition to improving our relationships, this mindset can reduce a significant amount of unnecessary stress and conflict in our lives. So much of the time, we work ourselves up over things that have little to do with us. We ruminate on what someone said or did, convinced that it's about us and our worth. But when we realize that others' behavior is often a reflection of themselves, we can let go of this burden. We can stop wasting energy on trying to control or change others and instead focus on what we can control – our own reactions and responses.

Advice From Someone That Loves You:

I don't want you to ignore our own needs and feelings. It's is difficult sometimes to recognize that we are not the center of everyone else's universe. It's about cultivating empathy, understanding, and patience in our interactions with others. And it's about freeing yourself from the stress and anxiety of taking everything so personally. By embracing this concept, you can create more positive, compassionate, and peaceful relationships – and live a less reactive, more meaningful life.

I HOPE YOU HAVE LEARNED

Choose To Be Kind, Even When It's Not Easy

Kindness. Such a simple word, yet with a weight that can move mountains. It costs nothing, but its impact is immeasurable. Picture this. You're in the middle of a crowded campus coffee shop, running on four hours of sleep, a questionable energy drink, and sheer willpower. You're waiting for your overpriced latte, desperately trying to remember the difference between "mitosis" and "meiosis" because there's a quiz in an hour. Suddenly, someone cuts in front of you in line. No apology. No acknowledgment. Just... right there. Kindness is probably the last thing on your mind in that moment. And honestly, who could blame you? It's so easy to react. Shoot an icy glare, roll your eyes, mutter something under your breath loud enough for them to hear. Or maybe just stew in silence and spend the rest of your day replaying the situation in your head. But what if you didn't? What if, instead of letting the frustration brew like that latte you're waiting for, you chose to be kind?

The thing about kindness is that it doesn't just happen. It's a choice. A deliberate decision to act with grace and patience, even when you don't feel like it. Especially when you don't feel like it. Being kind doesn't mean agreeing with someone cutting in line or pretending it's okay when someone is rude. It's about rising above those feelings and choosing how you react, not because of who they are, but because of who you are. Kindness isn't about them; it's about you.

Life is stressful, and everyone's carrying something you can't see. Exams, family stuff, relationships, money problems. The person who just cut in line? Yeah, sure, they might just be rude. Or, maybe they're distracted because they just bombed a test or got bad news from home. Your small act of kindness could be a reminder that the world isn't entirely terrible. And here's the wild part—it doesn't just make them feel good. Choosing kindness actually makes you feel good, too. Studies show that kindness has all sorts of benefits, from reducing stress to boosting your mood. Basically, choosing to be kind is like giving yourself a little mental high-five. Alright, so how do you actually do this whole kindness thing? Here are some starter ideas:

- When someone bumps your arm in the hallway or accidentally nudges your stuff off the table, resist the urge to give them a stink eye. Instead, smile (even a small one counts) and say, "No worries." Nine times out of ten, they'll relax and thank you. You've made their day a little easier, and maybe yours too.
- Compliment someone out of the blue. Notice a cool hoodie? Love their backpack? Tell them! It's super low effort and will probably make them smile all day.
- This is a big one. Kindness doesn't mean letting people take advantage of you or pretending you're okay when you're

not. It's saying "no" respectfully, giving constructive feedback nicely, or addressing frustrating situations with patience.
- When you finally get that latte, say "thank you" like you mean it. Baristas see dozens of rushed, stressed-out people every day. A little kindness can make you stand out—in a good way.
- When someone cuts in line, sends a confronting text, or gets under your skin, take a beat. Just one second to breathe and decide how you want to respond. Remember, being kind doesn't mean stuffing your feelings down; it just means handling them thoughtfully.

Spoiler alert: you're going to mess this up. You're human. Some days you'll snap or say something snarky, and that's okay. Kindness isn't about being perfect; it's about trying. If you mess up, apologize and move forward. And here's the thing about kindness—it's catchy. When you choose to respond with kindness, it often inspires the same in others. It's like one of those chain reactions in chemistry (except, you know, with fewer explosions). You have no idea how far a simple act of kindness can ripple. Today, it could be a smile or a calm reaction; tomorrow, it could inspire them to pay it forward.

College and life after high school are tough. There's no manual for navigating all the random, chaotic situations you'll face. But here's a cheat code that works almost every time: choose to be kind. Not because it's easy, but because it matters. And trust us, it's worth it.

I hope you learn to be kind—not just to others, but to yourself as well. Being kind to others opens doors you didn't know existed. A smile, a thoughtful word, or a quiet moment of encouragement can completely transform someone's day. You hold the power to offer light in moments when someone else might be struggling through darkness. Do not underestimate the ripple effect of small, intentional acts of kindness. They echo farther than you will ever realize. But remember, kindness is also about extending grace to yourself. College life, deadlines, relationships—it's easy to feel like you're falling short. Pause. Take a breath. Bravery and effort deserve appreciation too, even if they only come in small steps. Speak to yourself as you would to a friend—with compassion.

Sometimes, life feels rushed, competitive, like a silent race to prove your worth through achievements. But kindness interrupts that heartbreakingly noisy rhythm. It reminds us that the true strength of our character is seen through how we treat others, especially when it's inconvenient, and how we nurture our own souls, especially when we feel unworthy. Today, take one small step toward kindness. Hold a door open. Say "thank you." Compliment someone you've never spoken to before, or listen to your inner voice and recognize your own hard work.Learning to be kind won't happen all at once, and that's okay. It's a practice, something you can weave into the everyday moments of your life. I hope you learn to bring kindness wherever you go. And in doing so, I hope you find just how much brighter the world, and your own heart, can be.

Advice From Someone That Loves You:

I remember times when people were not kind to you. I even remember times that I wish I had been more kind to you. We live in a world today where few people really wake up in the morning and make it a priority to be kind. You will come across people today that your kind word to them might be just what they need to keep going. You may be the only person that treats them with kindness and respect. How about trying today to be kind to someone who doesn't even deserve it. Just tell them that was the way you were raised.

I HOPE YOU HAVE LEARNED

Finishing What You Start, Is Important

You've probably heard it said, "It's not how you start, but how you finish." And it's true. Have you ever started something with the burning enthusiasm of someone who's just had their third cup of coffee, only to abandon it halfway through because, well… Netflix started asking if you're still watching? Be honest, we've all been there. Whether it's a group project, a new fitness plan, or that 10-week "Learn Spanish Fast" course you signed up for on a whim, sticking with commitments can feel hard. Often, what starts with excitement and high hopes ends with excuses and a sigh of, "I'll do it next week."

But here's the thing about unfinished business in life (and in faith): you miss out on God's lessons and blessings when you don't see things through. God calls us to do everything with excellence and perseverance—not just the exciting stuff, but the boring and tough things, too. Why? Because finishing what we start reflects discipline, grows our character, and glorifies Him. Jesus set the ultimate example of finishing what He started. He could have stopped at any time during His ministry or during His walk to the cross. But He didn't. He finished the mission God sent Him to accomplish —for you and for me.

Whether you're navigating college assignments or figuring out post-graduation life, remember this truth: God is shaping you through every task, every commitment, and every challenge. Even that midterm paper or family obligation that feels like pulling teeth has purpose. Seeing it through isn't just about ticking it off your to-do list; it's about growing into the person God is calling you to be. Picture this: you've signed up for a marathon. The starting line is buzzing with excitement, you're pumped up with adrenaline, and you cross that starting line with all the enthusiasm in the world. But halfway through the race, your legs feel like jelly, and the finish line seems impossibly far away. You think, "Why did I even start this? Maybe no one will notice if I sneak out now." Sound familiar?

While life isn't always a literal marathon, it sure can feel like one. College projects, job hunts, personal goals, relationships, dreams—we eagerly jump in with inspiration and energy, but often hit the "middle mile slump." The shiny excitement? Gone. All that's left is the hard work. Here's the thing though, the people and activities you admire most? They didn't just start strong; they *finished well*. The most powerful, impactful results often come when you push through that mid-point drag.

Starting something new often feels exciting—there's energy, motivation, and a clear sense of possibility. Whether it's a college semester, a new workout plan, or a personal goal, beginnings are filled with promise. But as time passes, challenges creep in, distractions surface, and staying committed becomes difficult. This is where the importance of finishing comes in. Starting alone doesn't bring fulfillment—it's the follow-through that matters. Imagine signing up for a marathon and quitting after the first mile. You wouldn't experience the joy and sense of accomplishment waiting at the finish line.

Think about your life right now. Maybe you're a college student working through finals, a young professional juggling responsibilities, or someone just trying to stay motivated in your daily grind. Whatever you're facing, remind yourself that finishing isn't just about persistence—it's about character. It shows you honor your commitments, even when it's tough. Finishing builds qualities that will support you throughout life—discipline, focus, and diligence. It teaches you how to find strength when motivation fades and how to prioritize what truly matters over fleeting distractions. Even when it feels difficult, completing what you've started brings purpose and growth. But finishing doesn't mean being perfect. It means doing your best with what you have, trusting that small, consistent efforts add up. Give yourself grace for mistakes, but don't give up. Push forward, knowing that every challenge you face equips you for something greater.

Today, take a moment to reflect on what you've started and haven't yet finished. What's one thing, big or small, that you can commit to completing? Don't settle for "almost"; step up and cross the finish line. Remember, the reward isn't just in reaching the end—it's in who you become along the way. Finishing is important. You've got this!

Advice From Someone That Loves You:

How many times were you told growing up to make sure that you finished what you started. Many times as adults we say that because we didn't finish things and we regret that we didn't. Now that you are on your own I hope you realize that people are often counting on you to do what you said you would do. They are looking to see exactly who you are on the inside. Sometimes what you need to finish isn't a big deal to you, but it is a very big deal to them.

I HOPE YOU HAVE LEARNED

It's Easy To Make A Bad Decision

Have you ever found yourself stuck between two paths, unsure which one to take? Life throws a lot of choices at us, especially during college or when you're fresh out of high school. What major should you choose? Should you join that club or try for the basketball team? Is eating cereal for dinner again a terrible idea? The truth is, making decisions can be HARD. And sometimes, it feels like no matter what you decide, there's a chance it might not go the way you planned. It's kind of like standing at a buffet with too many options. You grab the mysterious casserole, thinking it might be exotic and exciting, only to discover… it's tuna surprise. And not even the good kind.

Here's the thing about decisions: we're often tempted to choose what feels best in the moment, even if it's not what's best long-term. Why? Because our brains like shortcuts. And while shortcuts work in math exams (sometimes), they're tricky at avoiding regrets. Maybe you skipped studying for a test because Netflix was calling your name (and now *failing* is calling your name). Or maybe you said "yes" to something because of peer pressure when all you really wanted to do was say "no, thanks" and eat ice cream in your pajamas.

It's easy to fall into the instant gratification trap. But here's the good news! The fact that you're reading a devotional about decision-making shows you're already thinking about how to make better ones. That's half the battle won.

- Most bad decisions happen when you feel rushed. If someone asks you to make a big choice and your reply would normally be something like "Uh, sure, I guess???" take a breath. Good decisions need time, not panic mode.
- If you're eating Cheetos at 2 AM and thinking about switching your major to "Professional Memeology" because it sounds fun, you might need to sleep on it. But your instincts can be really helpful in guiding you toward choices that align with your values.
- Picture yourself two weeks (or years!) down the road after making a certain decision. Will future you be high-fiving past you or throwing side-eye at them?
- Your friends, mentors, or family might not have all the answers, but they often have perspectives you haven't thought about. Plus, they care about you and want to see you thrive.

Here's the part no one talks about enough: you WILL make bad decisions sometimes. And you know what? That's okay. Every single person does. Bad decisions are a part of growing up, growing wiser, and figuring out what works for you.

What matters is what you do after. Will you learn from it? Will you laugh about it (at least eventually)? Will you use it to make a better choice next time? Remember, even if you've taken a "wrong turn" somewhere, you're never stuck there forever. There's always a chance to correct, redirect, and move forward with a little more confidence. When it comes to navigating life's decisions, don't stress over the "perfect choice." Aim for the "best choice you can make with the info you've got" and go from there. College, post-high school life, or wherever you're at might feel overwhelming sometimes, but you're doing better than you probably realize. And, hey, if you mess up? That's what cereal for dinner is for. It won't solve everything, but it's a pretty great way to regroup.

Maybe it's choosing a college major, deciding whether to take an internship, or figuring out if a new friendship is worth pursuing. These moments of decision-making can feel overwhelming, especially when the answer isn't clear. This is where discernment comes in. Discernment isn't just about making "good" choices—it's about making the *right* ones for you. It's tuning into that still, quiet voice within you and learning to trust that sense of inner guidance. Discernment asks you to dig deep and seek clarity, not just from your own thoughts and experiences but by reflecting on what aligns with your values, goals, and ultimate vision for your life. Life is full of crossroads, and discernment doesn't promise easy answers. It calls for patience, self-awareness, and intentionality. Discernment is practiced by asking yourself questions like, "Does this align with the best version of myself?" or "How will this choice shape the person I want to become?" Building discernment takes time, but it starts with simple steps. Set aside a few quiet moments daily to reflect on your thoughts and decisions. Journal your feelings when faced with big choices. Surround yourself with wise and supportive people who challenge you to look at situations from different perspectives. College and young adulthood are exciting seasons. They're filled with opportunities to grow, build, and define your identity. But they're also a time when discernment becomes a needed skill in navigating life's challenges and changes. Take heart—learning discernment is a process. Trust yourself to make decisions that reflect your heart and values. Through reflection, practice, and faith, you'll gain the confidence to face even the most uncertain paths with clarity and purpose.

Advice From Someone That Loves You:

I know you make good decisions. However, I also know that yo have made some bad ones-we all have. We often make bad decisions even after we know it is not what we should do. But that is the way life is, we keep doing what we know we shouldn't do. Why? Because it often sounds like fun. Making good decisions is hard. Even when we make bad decisions, we sometimes make them believing they are good.

Don't get yourself down. You are smart and I am proud of you. Use your life experiences and pray for wisdom.

I HOPE YOU HAVE LEARNED

To Share, If You Have More Than Others

Have you ever paused to reflect on the blessings in your life—your time, talents, or even your material resources? It's easy to focus on what we lack, but how often do we stop to think about what we have in abundance?

Imagine this. You just snagged free pizza at a campus event. Life is good. On your way back to your dorm, pizza box in hand, someone from your hall glances at you with that unmistakable "please share" look. And maybe you hesitate for a moment, but then you think, "Eh, I've got more than enough." You hand over a slice, they light up, and suddenly, it feels like a better day—not just for them, but for you too. Sharing isn't hard when we know we have enough. The tricky part is recognizing that "enough" isn't just about stuff. Sometimes, it's about time, kindness, or even the random talents we've got tucked away. Whether it's tutoring a friend who's struggling with stats or just sharing Netflix logins (shh, I won't tell), you've got something someone else could use right now.

Here's the kicker, though. When you give, it's not just about helping others. It grows your heart, plain and simple. Think of it like a muscle. The more you flex that "generosity muscle," the stronger it gets. Little by little, giving shifts from, "Well, I guess I could spare this..." to, "Who else can I help today?" It's wild how that works.

And sharing doesn't have to be a grand gesture. Some of the best, most impactful acts of generosity cost you nothing. Got time to send someone a playlist of fresh beats? Do it. Know someone spiraling before finals? Go get coffee with them—even if they just rant about their professors the whole time. You don't have to lead a canned food drive tomorrow to make this real. Start small. Think about what you have more of than others right now. Maybe it's wisdom about where to get the best free food on campus, or an extra jacket you never wear. Maybe it's just a good word someone's dying to hear—that "You've got this" nobody else is saying.

Because here's the deal. When you share *anything* you've got more of, the world changes. Not all at once, not in flashy ways—but for that person, in that moment, it does. And trust me, that's enough to make a pizza slice worth giving. Go share something today. You've got more of it than you think.

Imagine this. You have two sandwiches, but the person beside you hasn't eaten all day. It's a small example, but the principle is powerful. When you have more than you need, it's an opportunity to share. Sharing isn't just about material things; it's also about our time and energy. When you stay up late explaining a math concept to a struggling friend, you're sharing your knowledge. When you lend someone a listening ear during a tough moment, you're giving them comfort. But why does sharing feel so significant? Because it's not just about the person receiving; it's about the impact giving has on you. Generosity plants seeds of gratitude in your own heart. It builds stronger bonds with those around you and reminds you of the joy that exists in being part of a bigger, interconnected world. As college students and young adults, you're in a season where resources might feel tight—money, time, and even energy can often seem limited. But even in these moments, there's always something you can give. It could be sharing notes from a class, offering encouragement to a classmate after a tough exam, or inviting someone who's feeling lonely to sit with your group. Consider this as you go about your week. Where do you have *more*? What can you share with someone else? The smallest act of kindness can brighten someone's day—and you'll often find that it brightens yours too. Your generosity matters, and it leaves a mark. Remember, even what seems small to you can mean the world to someone else.

Advice From Someone That Loves You:

You may not have as much as you wish you had, but I promise that you have more than many. We often find ourselves participating in the comparison drama of life. We look at others and make a decision on how little we have in comparison. However, as you know, that can work the other way as well. You will find on many occasions that you have more than many around you. It's really not your own possessions because you have been give them by others. I promise you this, you will love giving aways things more than getting them.

I HOPE YOU HAVE LEARNED

To Be Content, With What You Have

It's tempting to always want more, isn't it? Another A on your report card. A bigger apartment. The latest phone. Social media seems to constantly remind us of what we *don't* have—what others are achieving, buying, or experiencing. But here's something beautiful to remember, especially as you step into adulthood and build your dreams: contentment is a choice, not a destination. Being content doesn't mean you stop striving for improvement. It doesn't mean settling or dismissing ambition. Instead, it's learning to appreciate the blessings right in front of you while working toward your future goals.

Have you noticed how easy it is to fall into the comparison trap? Especially in college, or after high school, when you're surrounded by people showing off their latest gadgets, posting vacation pics from tropical getaways, or talking about their seemingly perfect internships. It's everywhere, isn't it? Instagram, TikTok, your group chat… Sometimes it feels like everyone around you is living their best life while you're over here wondering if ramen for dinner *again* is acceptable. (Spoiler alert: it totally is.)

Here's the thing about chasing what others have—it's exhausting. You'll get caught up trying to "keep up," but you won't feel fulfilled. Instead, you'll end up overwhelmed, stressed, and frustrated because newsflash: there's *always* going to be someone who seems to have more.

But here's the beauty of contentment. When you take a moment to pause and appreciate what's already in your life, everything changes. Contentment flips the script. It reminds you to find joy in the little things, like late-night laughs with friends, that well-worn hoodie that feels like a warm hug, or the way the campus glows when the sun sets.

It doesn't mean you shouldn't set goals or want nice things someday. Dream big! Chase those ambitions! But at the same time, don't overlook the blessings you already have. When you learn to be content with what's in front of you, you'll find a sense of peace that shiny new things can't buy. Here's a challenge for today (don't worry, it's easier than group projects): take five minutes to write down three things you're grateful for. Big or small, it doesn't matter. Reflect on why they matter to you. Gratitude has a funny way of making what you have feel like more than enough.

Remember, your worth isn't tied to what you own or where you've been. It's about who you are and the joy you bring into the world. Keep your eyes on your path, stop scrolling for someone else's highlight reel, and celebrate the richness of your unique, one-of-a-kind life. Because, friend, you're already enough. Right here. Right now.

Contentment is about shifting your focus. Have you eaten today? Does the sun come up where you live? Do you have a friend who can make you laugh so hard you cry? These moments and things may seem small in comparison to your aspirations, but they are gifts—precious glimpses of life's goodness. When you learn to be content, your heart becomes lighter. Stress starts to fade, replaced by a quiet joy. Instead of looking outward for what's missing, you'll find yourself looking inward, realizing how much you already possess. Contentment teaches you gratitude. And gratitude—the act of noticing and appreciating—opens the door for peace like nothing else. For the young adult navigating college, career, or relationships, learning this early will give you strength. Life will bring challenges, and yes, there will be setbacks. But if you can pause and find satisfaction in what you already have, you'll see there's beauty in every stage of your life, no matter how uncertain it feels. Today, take a moment to breathe deeply and reflect. Write down three things you're grateful for. Practicing contentment starts here—one step, one acknowledgment, one smile at a time. You are enough, and you have enough. Always.

Advice From Someone That Loves You:

I have always had a problems being content with what I have been given and I am not proud of that. I have so many great things in my life. One of them is you. I am so thankful that

God gave you to me. I hope you learn how to be content with whatever you have. God promised to always give you what you need, not what you want. Consider what you really have in life. Be thankful.

I HOPE YOU HAVE LEARNED

To Be Present, In The Moment

Life in early adulthood often feels like a whirlwind—assignments, social events, exams, work, and everything in between. It's easy to get so caught up in what's next that you miss what's right here, right now. But when was the last time you truly paused, breathed in the moment, and appreciated where you are? "Wherever you are, be all there." It's a simple quote by Jim Elliot that packs a punch, especially when life feels like a whirlwind of schedules, notifications, and endless to-do lists. If you're balancing college classes, part-time jobs, late-night pizza runs, and the occasional existential crisis, being present in the moment can feel like a luxury you just don't have time for.

But here's the thing: it's a skill that can change your life. Have you noticed how we tend to live in the next thing? "What's next on my schedule?" "What's the next exam I need to study for?" "What do I need to do to make sure I crush this interview?" It's like we're always zooming ahead, trying to win at life, but missing the game that's happening right now. Before you know it, that coffee break with a friend becomes a list of unchecked tasks in your head. The afternoon hike you planned gets overshadowed by the urge to check your emails. Even a once-in-a-lifetime moment, like walking across the stage at graduation, can feel like a blurry "checkbox" if you're already thinking about "what's next." Spoiler alert? The future isn't going anywhere—but this moment you're in now? It's never coming back.

Being present sounds great, but how do you actually do it? Start with these three tips:

- Just for a bit. Like, right now. Seriously, when was the last time you walked across campus without scrolling? Try keeping your phone in your bag during lunch, or turning off notifications for an hour while you study. It's wild how much background noise clears up when you unplug.
- This might sound cheesy, but try it anyway. Feel the warmth of the sunshine when you're walking to class. Listen to someone's laugh and really soak it in. Focus on the smell of coffee brewing while you wait in line. These moments are small, but they're what make life *feel* alive.
- Multitasking is overrated. You might think you're a productivity ninja, but your brain isn't designed to do homework, check emails, and watch Netflix at the same time. Choose one task, do it well, and then move on to the next. Quality over quantity, always.

Life isn't a race to the finish line. It's a collection of moments, and the only way to truly *live* is to show up in each one. Laugh at the inside jokes. Taste the coffee. Cheer at the basketball game like you don't have finals next week. These are the moments you'll look back on one day—not what grade you got on your chem test or how perfect your group essay was. *Wherever you are, be all there.* It's not just a nice idea. It's the secret to experiencing life—not just passing through it. Now, your move. What's one thing you can do today to be more present? Go do it. (And yeah, we see you reaching for your phone to make a note—but AFTER you finish reading this. Be here now.)

Cell phone down, for a minute. Being present—it sounds simple, but it's something many of us struggle to do. Our minds are so often tied to the "when I...". *When I finish this semester, I'll be happy. When I land that job, I'll finally feel accomplished.* While these thoughts can be motivating, they rob us of the beauty and lessons of the present moment. The truth is, every day holds something sacred if we're willing to notice it. The smile of a friend, the satisfaction of completing that tough project, or even the peaceful silence of a morning walk—each moment is a gift. Learning to be present allows us to experience life fully, to find joy in the seemingly small things, and to grow in gratitude for where we are today. How can you practice being present when life feels overwhelming? Start small. When you're with a friend, focus on the conversation instead of checking your phone.

Take five minutes in the morning to reflect on what you're thankful for. Breathe. Pause when you're stressed, and center yourself in the here and now. Remember, life isn't just the milestones—it's the steps in between, the everyday moments that shape who we are. When you allow yourself to be fully present, you open your heart to growth, connection, and the peace that comes from savoring each day as it unfolds. Take a moment today to slow down and truly *be*. The present is waiting for you.

Advice From Someone That Loves You:

OK, turn off your cell phone and stop checking Facebook and Twitter. Live is passing by and I don't want you to miss it because you were not present in the moment. Great things are happening all around you and you need to be a part of them. The next time you are spending time with someone, be present. Don't allow the things in this world to side track you from the opportunities God has placed in your path.

I HOPE YOU HAVE LEARNED

Look For The Best, In Everyone

One of the greatest lessons you can learn in life is to see the goodness in others. It's not always easy—people are complex, and sometimes their flaws seem louder than their virtues. But when we make an effort to look past the surface, we uncover something truly remarkable.

Have you ever noticed how some people seem to go through life like a human highlighter? They're the ones who, no matter the situation, always manage to find the good in others. Whether it's the friend who cheers on everyone in the group chat or the professor who compliments your handwriting even when your essay bombed, these people seem to have a magical ability to see the best in everyone.

But here's the thing—you can be that person too. It's easy to focus on what's wrong with people. Maybe a classmate never shows up for their part of the group project, or your roommate leaves dirty dishes in the sink... again. It's human nature to notice the annoying or frustrating parts of others. But what if we tried to flip the script? The truth is, everyone has something good worth seeing. Maybe that classmate struggles with time management but has killer creative ideas. Or maybe your roommate is the best person to have deep talks with when life gets tough. Choosing to look for the good doesn't excuse the flaws, but it shifts your perspective.

When you make a habit of looking for the best in others, two things happen. First, people notice. They'll feel seen, appreciated, and valued. Second, it changes you. Suddenly, you're not just dealing with frustrating people or tough situations. You're seeing the potential and beauty in others, even during their not-so-great moments. Here's a fun challenge you can try this week: every day, find one good thing about someone around you. Tell your friend they have the coolest music taste. Compliment that fellow student who always asks thoughtful questions in class. Thank the dining hall worker who smiles at you every morning.

You might be surprised how much brighter the world seems when you start looking for the best in others. That small shift in mindset? It's more powerful than you think. You just might inspire others to do the same. Go ahead—be a human highlighter. The world really needs more of those.

The truth is, everyone carries their own burdens, battles, and untold stories. What if you chose to believe in the best version of them? What if, instead of focusing on their shortcomings, you decided to see their strengths, their kindness, or even just the potential that lies within them? When you shift your perspective, it changes more than just how you see other people—it changes how you live. Looking for the best in others builds stronger relationships, fosters trust, and creates a sense of community. People are more likely to rise to the expectations you set, and your belief in them often inspires them to believe in themselves. It also frees you from carrying the weight of grudges or frustration. When you choose grace over judgment, you open your heart to peace. Instead of allowing negativity to take root, you fill that space with understanding and compassion. Today, I challenge you to look for the good in someone around you. Maybe it's a classmate in your group project, someone who always tests your patience, or even a stranger you pass on your way to class. Choose to see them in a new light— perhaps someone who's trying, growing, and deserving of kindness. The world needs more people who seek out the best in others. Be that person. And in doing so, you'll find your own faith in humanity growing stronger, your relationships deepening, and your heart becoming a little lighter. Remember, looking for the best in everyone isn't about ignoring flaws; it's about choosing hope, choosing love.

Here's a little experiment for you today. Think of someone you find difficult to deal with (we all have *that* person). Then, instead of focusing on what's frustrating about them, take a moment to find one thing you admire or appreciate about them. It could be their effort, their work ethic, or even just how they showed up today. Not easy, right? But keep at it. The more you look for good, the more good you'll find—not just in others, but in yourself, too.

Advice From Someone That Loves You:

It's sometimes hard to find the good is some people. They act like jerks and they don't seem to want or have friends. However, everyone was created to be loved and to be special it is your job to find out how. Look past their faults and try to find what their talents and gifts really are. Isn't it hard to believe that everyone has a sweet spot. Everyone has a need to be loved. It is our job to break through the facade and find the real person.

I HOPE YOU HAVE LEARNED

To Admit, When You Are Wrong

Admitting when you're wrong isn't easy. It can feel uncomfortable, humbling, and at times even scary. But it's also one of the most important skills you can develop as a young adult. Why? Because owning up to your mistakes isn't a sign of weakness—it's a sign of growth, maturity, and strength.

Alright, let's be real for a second. Nobody *likes* being wrong. It's awkward. It's uncomfortable. And if you grew up with siblings, it probably came with a side of "I told you so." But here's the truth: messing up is part of being human, and admitting it? That's where the magic happens. We're all going to have moments where our words sting, our actions disappoint, or our decisions miss the mark. Maybe you forgot your best friend's birthday, or you didn't follow through on a promise. It doesn't feel great—but guess what? Admitting you're wrong isn't a sign of weakness. It's one of the strongest moves you can make. Here's why owning up is so powerful:

- It builds trust. When you're honest about your mistakes, people notice. It shows you care about the relationship more than your ego. Trust me, your friends, teammates, bosses, or professors will respect your honesty a whole lot more than watching you awkwardly double down or make excuses.

- It's freeing. Ever feel that weight in your chest after messing up? That's guilt. And it's heavy. Admitting you're wrong helps lift that burden. It's like a reset button for your heart and your head.

- It shows you're still growing. Spoiler alert: nobody expects you to have it all figured out in your teens or twenties. When you admit you're wrong, you're proving that you're willing to learn, grow, and evolve. And honestly? That kind of self-awareness will get you further in life than pretending you've got it all together.

We're all figuring it out as we go. But when you can drop the act, admit you're human, and commit to doing better, you'll find that people are a whole lot more forgiving than you think. And who knows, the next time you hear a friend admit they're wrong, you might surprise yourself by saying, "It's all good. Same boat, remember?"

Think about it. Nobody is perfect. We all make mistakes, say things we don't mean, or take actions we later regret. The real question isn't whether or not we mess up—it's how we respond when we do. Do we brush it off, point fingers, or make excuses? Or do we take a deep breath, step into accountability, and admit, "I was wrong"? Admitting fault creates space for healing and deepens your relationships. Your friends, classmates, or even professors will respect your honesty far more than any attempt to cover up a mistake.

Instead of losing trust, you actually build it by showing you value integrity over pride. But this isn't just about relationships with others—it's also about your relationship with yourself. When you take responsibility for your actions, you open the door to personal growth. You learn from your experiences, identify areas where you can improve, and prepare yourself to handle things better in the future. It's okay to be wrong. It's okay to not have all the answers. What's not okay is letting pride keep you stuck in denial when you know you need to take accountability. Today, take a moment to reflect. Is there anyone you owe an apology to? A moment where you could have said, "That's on me"? If so, it's not too late to make things right. Growth starts when humility steps in. Take the first step. You'll be better for it.

Advice From Someone That Loves You:

Saying I am sorry is tough. I know many times I have missed the opportunity to do the right thing. Admitting when we are wrong is often difficult and you probably got that through the gene pool. If it was hard for me then I know it was probably hard for you. People admire those that are honest and fess up when they make mistakes. If you want to be admired by your friends, be the first one to say I am sorry. Many great relationships have been ruined because people were to proud to say I was wrong

I HOPE YOU HAVE LEARNED

How To Say, I Am Sorry

Life is full of moments where mistakes are made—by us and by those around us. It's easy to focus on the mistakes of others, to point fingers, or to justify our own actions. But what if the most powerful words we can say aren't about explaining ourselves, but humbly acknowledging our shortcomings?

We've all been there. That awkward moment when we know we messed up, and we need to face the person we hurt. Maybe you overreacted in the group project. Maybe you broke a promise. Or maybe you borrowed (read: stole) your roommate's last slice of pizza at midnight. Whatever the situation, saying "I'm sorry" can feel like trying to run a marathon without any training. Exhausting. Awkward. Hard to start. But here's the truth—even the best of us get it wrong sometimes. Apologies aren't meant to highlight our failures; they're about owning up, making things right, and showing that we value the people around us. Here's a step-by-step guide on how to say, "I'm sorry," without it feeling like pulling teeth.

- Pause for a Minute. Before you rush in guns blazing with an apology, take a breather. Use this time to really think about what happened. Why are you feeling sorry? Reflect on the situation and the role you played. Was it your tone? Your choice of words? Not returning that borrowed hoodie for six months? The goal here is clarity, not overthinking.

- Be Specific. People can sense when you're just throwing "sorry" around like confetti. A meaningful apology is in the details. If you ate your roommate's pizza, don't just say, "Sorry I ate your food." Say, "I'm sorry I ate your last slice of pizza, even though I know you were saving it. That wasn't cool of me." Specificity shows that you're paying attention and that you're actually invested in making things right.

- Acknowledge Their Feelings. Apologies aren't just about you and what you did; they're about the person on the other side of the situation. Acknowledge how they may have felt because of your actions.

- Offer to Make Amends. A genuine apology doesn't just clear the air; it's backed up by action. Ask what you can do to make it right, or suggest something yourself. Even small gestures show that your apology isn't just words, but the beginning of a positive change.

Learning to say, "I'm sorry," is one of the hardest lessons in life. It demands vulnerability, humility, and courage—qualities that are sometimes in short supply, especially when pride takes over or when fear of rejection holds us back. Apologizing begins with self-awareness. It's about recognizing when your words hurt or your actions caused pain. It's not about who was "more wrong" but about taking responsibility for your part, no matter how small it may seem. A sincere "I'm sorry" acknowledges the worth of the other person and validates their feelings. It says, "You matter to me. I value this relationship enough to mend what's been broken." But there's beauty in this. Saying "I'm sorry" doesn't just heal them—it heals you, too. It lifts the weight of regret, melts away misunderstandings, and restores peace to your heart. It's a bold declaration that relationships are more important than being right.

To the college students and young adults reading this, know that learning to apologize is one of the most courageous things you'll do. It's not weakness; it's strength. It builds character, strengthens relationships, and reflects love and grace. If you've been carrying guilt or waiting for the "perfect moment" to apologize to someone—don't wait any longer. Pick up your phone, write that text, or have that face-to-face conversation. You may be surprised at how freeing those two small words, "I'm sorry," can truly be. You have the power to mend what's been broken. Use it.

Advice From Someone That Loves You:

If I ever disappointed you, I want you to know that I am sorry. Saying I am sorry is important but often hard to do. Saying I'm sorry isn't just about admitting fault—it's about rebuilding trust, showing humility, and strengthening relationships. It takes courage, but a sincere apology can heal wounds and bring peace to your heart. Remember, owning your mistakes is a step toward growth and deeper connections with others.

I HOPE YOU HAVE LEARNED

To Live For What Lasts

It's easy to chase fleeting things—accomplishments, possessions, applause. But my prayer is that you focus on what truly matters. Congratulations! Whether you've just finished high school or gotten your first taste of college life, you've reached an exciting chapter. The possibilities are endless, and the world feels wide open. But with all these new experiences, decisions, and responsibilities, you might also be asking, "What really matters? What should I focus on?"

Here's the thing about this season of life: everything feels urgent. Deadlines, relationships, grades, career choices, friends, social events… somewhere in that whirlwind, it's easy to lose sight of the bigger picture. What is it that truly lasts? Spoiler alert: It's not your trending playlist, the double latte you Insta-storied, or even (brace yourself) your GPA. Sure, those things matter to an extent. But they're temporary. And you weren't created for temporary. You were created for a purpose that goes beyond what you can see, swipe, or like. Living for what lasts is about focusing on what has eternal value. It's investing in people, not just followers. It's choosing character over convenience, roots over quick wins. It's about being bold enough to ask yourself three big questions:

- What am I building? Think about each choice you're making like bricks in a wall. Are you building something strong and meaningful, or just something shiny and trendy? Brick by brick, your habits and priorities are creating the foundation of your life.

- Who am I becoming? The most important thing you bring into the world isn't your resume or credentials. It's *you.* Your values, your character, and how you treat others will be what people remember long after the accolades.
- How am I impacting others? Your time, your energy, your conversations matter. Even a small act of kindness can ripple into someone's life in ways you may never see. And when you choose to lead with love, you're investing in what outlives you.

Does this mean you need to quit studying or stop going to game nights with friends? Of course not. But it does mean pausing every so often to ask yourself, "Am I living for what's going to fade away, or for what's going to last?" The best news? You don't have to figure it all out today. Step by step, decision by decision, you get to build a life that matters, one rooted in something greater than the chaos of deadlines and societal expectations. And when you do, you'll find yourself chasing less of what's temporary and stepping fully into the purpose and meaning you were created for. That's the kind of life that lasts. So go ahead, take the next small step that leads to something bigger. You're meant for it.

Value relationships over recognition, character over convenience, love over status. Life is short, but the seeds of faith, love, and integrity you plant will echo into eternity.

Every moment of our lives, we're faced with choices about where to invest our time, energy, and attention. Social media, classes, friendships, and even career aspirations can pull us in countless directions. But here's a tough question to ask yourself today—are the things you're living for going to last? Think about it. Many of the things we chase after—likes on Instagram, the fleeting approval of others, or even trying to be "perfect" in everything—lose their shine over time. They don't bring the deep fulfillment we expected. It's like filling a cup with holes. No matter how much you pour in, it's never enough.

Living for what lasts means focusing on things with eternal significance, things that bring long-term meaning. Start with relationships. Invest in the people who truly care about you, who make you better, and whom you can pour into as well. Say "yes" to experiences that shape your character, teach you resilience, and strengthen your spirit. Also, reflect on the purpose behind what you do. Studying hard or working towards a dream isn't just about ticking boxes or pleasing others. It's about growing into who you're meant to be, not just achieving some arbitrary end. To live for what lasts also means tuning into your inner calling—listening to what truly inspires and fulfills you. Remember, you don't have to have everything figured out today. What matters is the direction you're heading. Each day brings another chance to align your life with purpose, growth, and love. Take a moment today to pause and ask yourself, "Am I living for what truly matters?"

It's a small step, but answering honestly could change everything.

Advice From Someone That Loves You:

Life moves fast, with so many distractions pulling at your attention. But pause and ask yourself—what will truly matter years from now? Invest your energy into lasting relationships, meaningful work, and personal growth. Focus on the things that build character and bring joy that endures. Avoid chasing fleeting trends or temporary approval. Instead, live intentionally, seeking purpose in what stands the test of time. Today's small choices can shape a legacy that lasts far beyond you.

I HOPE YOU HAVE LEARNED

Make Time To Rest And Relax

The world will whisper, "Do more. Achieve more." But even Jesus took time to step away and rest. Between late-night cram sessions, back-to-back assignments, and part-time jobs, it can feel like life never lets you off the hook. Who has time to rest when there's always another deadline lurking around the corner? But here's the truth you may need to hear today: rest isn't optional, it's essential. Think of yourself as a phone. Your body and mind are your hardware, and your energy? That's your battery. Now, what happens when you run your phone on 2% battery all day? Apps crash, functions slow down, and eventually, no matter how much you press the power button, it shuts off. That's what happens when you ignore rest. You can't run on empty forever.

You might think, "I'm young! I'll rest after finals...or this internship...or, well, someday." But here's the kicker—that "someday" will keep moving if you don't make rest a priority now. Rest doesn't just mean sleep (though, hey, those 4-hour nights aren't helping). It means taking intentional breaks to recharge, whether that's a walk outside, binge-watching your favorite show guilt-free, or just sitting in silence with your thoughts.

Relaxation isn't lazy; it's productive. Clearing your mental clutter makes room for creativity, focus, and clarity. If you want to give your best to your dreams and goals, you need to give yourself the permission to pause. You'll find that even a 30-minute breather can turn your day around. Here's a challenge for you today: schedule time to just *be*. Not time to task-switch between studying and scrolling TikTok. Not hanging out while still stressing over that group project. I mean real, purposeful downtime. Think of it as charging your inner battery. Because when it's fully charged? You're unstoppable. Take this as your sign to pause, breathe, and unplug for a while. You've earned it, and you deserve it.

Make room for moments of peace—unhurried conversations with God, quiet walks, or heartfelt prayers. These pauses will keep your heart aligned with His wisdom and your energy ready for life's demands. Life can feel incredibly demanding at times, especially when you're balancing classes, part-time jobs, and social commitments. It's easy to get caught up in thinking you always need to be doing something productive or staying busy. But the truth is, rest isn't a luxury—it's a necessity. When we push ourselves to the limit, we risk burnout. That constant hustle can drain not only your energy but also your sense of joy and purpose. The most meaningful accomplishments won't feel fulfilling if they come at the expense of your well-being. That's why taking time to rest and relax is so important. Think of rest as a reset button. It helps you refocus, recharge, and return to your responsibilities with a clear mind and a renewed spirit.

Taking intentional downtime—whether that's a quiet cup of coffee in the morning, a long walk in the park, or even a soothing playlist in the evening—can work wonders for both your mental and physical health. Remember, rest doesn't mean laziness. It doesn't mean you're unproductive or lacking drive. Rest is what equips you to show up as your best self when it matters most. Start small. Look at your schedule and identify opportunities to pause. Set boundaries where you need to. Maybe it's saying "no" to one more Zoom call or stepping away from your textbooks for an hour to sit in stillness. Allow yourself to breathe. And while you relax, be fully present. No guilt, no distractions. Rest should feel like an act of self-care, not something you have to earn. Today, I encourage you to intentionally set aside a moment for rest. Protect that time and use it to recharge—mind, body, and soul. Rest is how we honor ourselves and show gratitude for the strength we've been given.

Advice From Someone That Loves You:

Life moves fast, but don't forget the importance of rest. Taking time to relax isn't a luxury—it's essential for your well-being. Pause to recharge your mind, body, and spirit. Even a moment of stillness helps you refocus and find peace amidst the chaos. Put down the to-do list, step away from the noise, and give yourself permission to simply breathe. Rest renews your strength and prepares you for what's ahead. Today, choose to prioritize rest—you deserve it.

I HOPE YOU HAVE LEARNED

To Remember, You Are Never Alone

Life often feels like a mix of joy, challenge, and uncertainty, doesn't it? Especially for young adults, navigating college, friendships, and future plans can lead to moments of doubt and loneliness. It's in these moments that the simple truth bears repeating—you are never alone. Picture this. It's your first week away from home. The dorm room still smells like yesterday's pizza, your roommate has already claimed the better side of the room, and you can't quite figure out which way is north on campus (seriously, why isn't there a map with YOU ARE HERE on every corner?). Sound familiar?

Whether you're stepping into the whirlwind of college or finding your way after high school, life can sometimes feel like you're on an island. A deserted one. With no cell service. But here's the truth—even on the days when it feels like no one gets you, when friends are busy or far away, or when you're battling your own doubts about the future, you are *never* truly alone. Why? Because connection isn't just about proximity, it's about purpose. Your life carries weight. There are people in this world made better just by your presence— even if you haven't met them yet.

Think about this moment in time. Whether you're sitting in a too-small dorm chair, commuting to work, or curled up in your childhood bedroom scrolling TikTok way past bedtime, you were designed with intention. You're not alone by accident, and you're certainly not facing life's chaotic twists and turns without hope.

Don't underestimate the power of reaching out. Maybe it's texting that friend you haven't spoken to since high school, taking a chance and showing up to the campus event you almost bailed on, or even saying "hi" to someone in your 8 a.m. lecture. Connection often begins where courage meets kindness. And hey, while you're at it, remember to give *yourself* some grace. Life gets messy. Decisions about majors, career paths, or what to have for lunch today can be overwhelming (hint, tacos). But the best part about this chapter of your life? You have so much time to figure it out.

Take heart in this truth as you face the day ahead, no matter what it holds. You are never alone, and you were *never* meant to do life alone. Even in tough moments, you are part of something bigger, woven into a larger story that holds loads of potential for joy, adventure, and maybe even the best tacos you've ever tasted. When life feels overwhelming, remember this simple mantra to carry with you like your favorite playlist on repeat: You matter. You belong. You are never alone. Your story has only just begun. Grab an extra slice of pizza, call a friend, and breathe. You've got this.

It's easy to believe the lie that no one understands what you're going through. Maybe your friends don't seem to notice your struggles, or it feels like everyone else has life figured out except for you. But isolation, though it feels real, is rarely the full story. There is always someone who cares, someone ready to stand with you, listen to you, and walk alongside you. Start by reaching out—to friends, mentors, or family. A short text, a coffee invite, or sharing how you're feeling can open doors to connection. You might be surprised how willing others are to step in when they know you're seeking support. Another practical step? Find a community where you feel at home. Whether it's a campus group, a coffee night with friends, or a club where shared passions bring people together, connection creates reassurance that you're part of something greater than yourself.

Most importantly, remind yourself daily that your worth isn't tied to external achievements or fleeting friendships. You are uniquely and wonderfully made, valuable beyond measure. Even in moments when life feels quiet or overwhelming, the peace and strength to continue remain within you. Today, take a moment to consider this: Whom can you talk to? What activity makes you feel connected? By simply allowing yourself to be seen and known, you'll experience the truth—you are never alone. Recharge, reconnect, and remember to care for yourself on this beautiful and personal journey ahead. You've got this, and there's a full community ready to stand with you.

Advice From Someone That Loves You:

Life can feel overwhelming, especially when you're navigating newfound independence. But even in moments when loneliness hits hardest, remember this truth—you are never truly alone. There's strength in reaching out—to friends, mentors, family and most of all grandparents. Finding connection might take courage, but the support waiting for you can feel life-changing. Most importantly, know there's a deeper presence walking alongside you through every challenge and triumph. Take comfort in that constant companionship. Lean into it, speak openly, and trust that you're held, even when it feels like no one else notices. You are seen. You are loved.

WHAT I HOPE YOU HAVE LEARNED

These experiences, hopes, and lessons aren't just a checklist—they are aspirations that can lead you toward a life filled with meaning, joy, and the presence of God in every step. The beauty of life is in the weaving together of triumphs, challenges, laughter, and quiet moments of reflection. Through every season, you will discover just how deeply you are loved and how impactful your life can be when aligned with purpose and faith. What are the things YOU hope to experience or pass on to your loved ones? May your life be rich with experiences and blessings, and may your heart stay open to never stop seeking, growing, and loving.

Whether you're celebrating victories or walking through valleys, you are deeply loved by the Creator of the universe. His plans for you are good, even when the path feels unclear. Lean on Him, trust in His promises, and look for His guidance in every season. My hope for you isn't that you live a perfect life. It's that you live a life full of faith, love, and courage, holding onto the truth that God is with you every step of the way. Whatever storms may come, may you stand firm, rooted in the hope that can only be found in Him.

You are loved.

About the Author

Dr. Pettigrew received his undergraduate degree at the University of Tennessee, his Master's degree at Murray State University, and his Doctoral degree from the University of Memphis.

Joe has been a high school teacher, university professor, College Dean, and the CEO for Leaderpoint Consulting Group. He has consulted with many of the most successful corporate leaders in the world and has close ties with many national Christian sports celebrities.

In 2008 he founded the national men's ministry, In The Zone. The ministry held in large arenas and churches was closed during Covid-19.

Joe has authored numerous books. He has been married to Trudy for over 50 years, and together they have three children: Ashley, Tara, and Tyler. He also has seven grandchildren.

Thanks for reading *Lessons I Hope You Have Learned.*

Joe@joepettigrew.org

May God Bless You.

www.ingramcontent.com/pod-product-compliance
Lightning Source LLC
Chambersburg PA
CBHW061255120726

48001CB00001B/308